GOD'S MANDATE FOR APOSTOLIC ORDER

DR ETHEL REID-SMITH

God's Mandate For Apostolic Order
"Understanding Kingdom Apostolic Order"

Dr Ethel Reid-Smith

DR ETHEL REID-SMITH

God's Mandate For Apostolic Order
Dr Ethel Reid-Smith

Published By Parables
December, 2018

All Rights Reserved. No part of this book may be reproduced or utilized in any form or by any means, electronic or mechanical, including photocopying, recording, or by any information storage and retrieval system, without permission in writing from the author.

    ISBN 978-1-945698-85-9
    Printed in the United States of America

Readers should be aware that Internet Web sites offered as citations and/or sources for further information may have been changed or disappeared between the time this was written and the time it is read.

FOREWORD

There is something that must be established at the start as you read this book, something vital. In the writing of and in the reading of a strong biblical work such as this, you and I, the readers, and Dr. Ethel Reid-Smith, the writer, bring certain ardent convictions with us. On some points, our convictions may be compatible. On other points, our convictions may differ. On still other points, our convictions may clash. This is the common experience of all people of faith. It seems that we can agree on many things but not all things.

Because this is so there is something that must be interjected at this point, some fundamental convictions that we embrace and bring with us to this work:

First, the Bible is Truth, God's Truth. It is Truth without any mixture of error. The Bible, and the Bible alone, is the standard of measure for all things pertaining to faith and practice – life and righteousness. People of biblical faith will embrace this fundamental conviction and be nurtured,, encouraged and challenged by what Dr. Ethel has written. People of unbelief will be challenged too – as they explore and examine their unbelief.

Second, people of biblical faith have *convictions*, strong convictions, built upon the Truth of God's Word. *God's Truth is greater than our convictions. Convictions* grip us. They give us spiritual backbone. They help us to stand in the midst of swirling theological controversy, troubling trials and adversity. Nevertheless, even though we value our *convictions* and, indeed, even though our *convictions* are valuable, God's Word, God's Truth, is greater than our *convictions.* Our *convictions* are subservient, always subservient, to the Truth of God's Word; not the other way around. The Truth – God's Word -- is the standard of measure – not our *convictions*. May you discern the difference and be transformed by the renewing of your mind as you read this book – and its vital interpretation of the fivefold ministries established by Christ for His church.

Third, proceeding from *convictions* are *principles. Convictions* grip us. *Principles* guide us. *Principles* add flavor, shape and color to our *convictions* and their expression in life and ministry.

Fourth, flowing out of our *principles* are *predilections* and *preferences, options* and *opinions* – and from all of these -- *choices* -- and, that is where the rubber meets the road: we make *choices* and *choices have consequences*. And, it is here, in the *consequences*, that our destinies are shaped and our testimonies are shared.

One potential consequence of your exposure to the truth contained is this book would be for you to sense that the time has arrived for you to discern, afresh and anew, the application of God's fivefold ministry for your life and ministry. I urge you to thoughtfully and prayerfully read this book, ever-seeking God's Truth. Travel with Dr. Ethel on an explorative journey to discover, develop and deploy the biblical application of God's five non-negotiable ministries for His church. Seek to ascertain a clear fresh, vision of what He is calling you to be and to do in the years immediately before you, your congregation and/or your small group. Pilgrimage together, as a congregation, or as a small group or as an individual seeking God's leadership.

Allow yourself to be guided by Christ to Seek then Shape then Share the fivefold ministries in your life, church or small group. Implement the fivefold ministries, intensely and intentionally, as operational goals to Guide the Actions, Govern the Activities and Guard the Attitudes of your congregation

And, finally, in closing, to Dr. Ethel Reid-Smith, may I pronounce a blessing. To you dear friend, I say, The noble saints of God salute you, and thank you, for this wondrous book, your gift to the Kingdom of God."

Dr. John Dee Jeffries
CEO / Acquisitions Editor; *Publish By Parables*
Senior Pastor, First Baptist Church, Chalmette, Louisiana

PREFACE

The Lord has been dealing with me for a number of years regarding His order for His church. This is just part of what the Lord desires His people to understand. He wants us to understand His Word, and know His purpose and desire, and the things that He seeks to accomplish in this last day by His Spirit. God wants His Church to be Apostolic with a Kingdom Purpose.

The goal of this book is to create stirring in the body of Christ into the awareness of the urgency and need to return to God's original plan for apostolic order in the body of Christ. It is very apparent that today's church is not the order God planned for the body of Christ on earth. The Spirit of God is shifting and shaking the foundation of what we believe for us to recognize that change is imminent. We as believers have a niche or function for a specific God given ministry. It is the responsibility of each believer to seek God's purpose and call for the edifying of the body. It is the responsibility of leadership to discern, equip and nurture believers for ministry. Many churches and their laity have become complacent and satisfied with being pew warmers. The Holy Spirit lies dormant within some of the believers who lack the power to pray or effect change in the lives of others. These Christians are carnal.

Some members of the body are operating in the five-fold ministry illegally. Without Apostolic authority, which is delegated to us by grace and the Holy Spirit, you are operating illegally. God desires His work on earth to be accomplished through the members of the body of Christ, the church. Many Christian organizations teach erroneous dogma and doctrine, and entrap the believers through witchcraft and the spirit of Jezebel. These organizations are not a part of God's original plan to develop mature Christians and evangelize the world. Even though some of these organizations are effective, there is still a gulf between the church and these groups that are doing the work of the church. Unfortunately, these organizations are using man's methods, power, and abilities, not God's.

Therefore, these organizations achieve very little for Him. God's plan is for His work to be accomplished through those that are His, not through organizations and ministries outside the principles of the Kingdom of God. This should be accomplished by the oversight of Spirit filled believers. The leadership of the church is accountable for the non-equipping of the saints. Therefore, leadership is responsible for the lack of interest and earnest endeavors to minister to the underprivileged as well as the underrepresented.

Even though, you might see redundant paragraphs, its only to reinforce a seed of knowledge to grow in the desire to decide to obey the command of God and do His mandate. You may not agree with my humble train of thought or philosophy, but you will be pulled into reexamining and rethinking your order as compared to God's Kingdom Apostolic order.

MANDATE

God is commanding those He is sending to the body of Christ to restore His Apostolic Order to the church. They are being commissioned by the Holy Spirit to teach, anoint, impart, authorize and send others to bring the believers back to God's original order for His church. From the ascension of Christ, to the early church, and the New Testament church, until now man has misinterpreted, and skewed what was revealed to the apostle Paul by the Holy Spirit concerning church order. The church is being shifted, and shaken into the awareness of the need to return to apostolic principles and practices. The correct understanding of what the church and its original apostolic purpose is what God is ordering for His church.

The apostle Paul was unreservedly committed to Christ and to the ministry of the gospel. He regarded himself as called to both his master's side and to the promulgation of the good news. This master disciple relationship between Jesus Christ and Paul, resulted in the revelation of the apostolic order for the church that was founded on Jesus being the chief corner stone and the teachings of the apostles and prophets. To better ascertain the concept of apostolic order, let's begin with the church.

The church is defined as hH KURIAKH EKKLHSIA, from Hebrew Q:HaL-YHWH: modern Hebrew Q:HiLaT-HaMMaiYaCh. The English took their word Church from KURIAKH, whereas the French took their word Eglise from EKKLHSIA, Latin ecclesia. Our word church derives from the Greek word Kyriakon, which is a name for the church building, John Ayto; Dictionary of Word Origins (Arcade: New York,

1990). Etymologically, a church is the Lord's house. Its ultimate source is the Greek kyrios. The adjective derived from this was kyriakos, whose use in the phrase, house of the Lord, led to its use as a noun, kyriakon. The medieval Greek form, kyrkon, house of worship, was borrowed from West Germanic as, kirika, which translated in German, kirche, and English, church. The Scots form, kirk, comes from Old Norse, kirkja, which was borrowed from Old English.

Howbeit, the church today has greatly deviated from God's intended apostolic order and has distorted the Jerusalem church example. The Church, if you take notice, was named for their geographical location, i.e., Jerusalem Church or Church at Antioch. God intended His church to be the Lord's house and a house of worship. The church today is competing with other members of the body instead of uniting as Christ prayed. It has lost its' credibility, and attraction to unbelievers. As Jesus went about preaching and teaching, the Pharisees and Sadducees who were steeped in the traditions of men, continued to challenge Jesus' authority. To spread the Gospel of Jesus Christ and salvation the Gospel must appeal to the masses and meet the needs of every soul that belongs to God. Salvation is a holistic and complete process that includes the spirit, soul, body, physical and material needs of the Saviors people. It seems as though various denominations or local churches are not interested in being accountable to the people they are serving, but rather in pursuing their own agenda. However, Ephesians the Fourth chapter describes God's intended apostolic order, and gives specific details to God's church. The message that Jesus taught was about God's Kingdom and His righteousness.

The church today tends to focus on evangelism overseas, rather than targeting or reaching out and advocating the rights of our youth, single parents, abortion, and the justice, education, government, and economic systems. By and large the world has regarded the church as an irrelevant waste of time. Because of these religious systems, (which consists of fanatics who are doing their own religious antics) the righteousness of God is being ignored. Even among those who are professing Christianity they are saying, "I'm a part of Christianity, but I want no part of churchianity." Within the body of Christ, believers have become discouraged and disenchanted with winning souls and doing what is right. One reason is due to of the lack of training, support, and teaching the truth within the church community. Charity begins at home, and then it should spread abroad. The leaders of local churches and denominations are responsible to the members and to God for the equipping, empowering, and releasing them to do the work of evangelizing. An effective leader's message should focus on Christ, the kingdom of God and His righteousness, as well as winning souls. By not doing so, the body of Christs' understanding of the sovereignty and the deity of Christ has become devalued and diminished. If Christ dwells in His people, then love shown to the body of believers, is an integral part of that communion with Christ which is eternal life.

When Christ prayed; "Lord make us one," he meant one body, not many denominations. William Seymour was the apostle of the Azusa Pentecostal movement. All the denominations that sprang from that movement formed their own niche within the body of that movement. Should all the board of leaders that make up all the heads of the denominations that were developed from that movement become one, that change would affect the body of Christ around the world. For one, the apostles did not form denominations. That was not their intent, their purpose was to spread the Gospel of Jesus Christ throughout the world, to spread the Word of God, not to add on or take away one jot or tittle.

The objective that Jesus has for His Church; make disciples of the nation, preach the Gospel to every creature, preach repentance and remission of sins, not just within the church or Christian community. When the full command is obeyed, the full promise will be fulfilled. We have become segmented and fragmented in our success for the unity of the body. We have become groupies with different rules, standards, protocols and procedures. The body of Christ is sick physically, relationally, spiritually, and financially. Over 85,000 or more people die daily without hearing the name Jesus.

Men have much doctrinal knowledge, yet are mere beginners in the life of faith, experience, and knowledge of the Kingdom of God and His righteousness. Contentions and quarrels about religion are sad evidences of carnality. True religion makes men peaceable, not contentious. (I Cor. 3:1-4). But it is to be lamented that many who should walk as Christians, live and act too much like men of the world. Many professors and preachers also, show themselves to be yet carnal, by vain-glorious strife, eagerness for dispute, readiness to despise and speak evil of others. This is called an intellectual spirit that comes when logic supersedes the wisdom of God.

Jesus Christ desires to establish His new testament church by giving five distinctly different types of calls or offices (five fold ministry, or offices: apostles, prophets, evangelists, pastors and teachers) not for control or member competition. He also imparts many varied gifts to Holy Spirit filled believers for the edification of the body of Christ. The called and anointed are to look to Jesus Christ for direction in their individual lives. They are then to serve the body in the way that Jesus directs them in right living and in truth. All members are equal and subservient to each other. The harmony of the body creates unity in the church, with all having one mind, one spirit, and one objective.

Just as there are certain necessary functions for the apostolic order of Christ, to some extent every Christian is responsible to carry out every one of these functions. But to each individual member of the body, God has given particular abilities to carry out some functions better than others. These abilities we call spiritual gifts.

Christ mandates social consciousness and concern. Here are principles by which men will be judged; their treatment of those who are hungry, homeless, poor, diseased, and imprisoned. Social concern cannot biblically be separated from the Christian walk. He who has pity on the poor lends to the Lord, and He will pay back what he has given (Prov. 19:17). Jesus equates our treatment of those who are destitute or distressed with our treatment of Himself. What we do for them, and other believers we do for Him.

The oneness Christ requests is not an organizational but a spiritual unity, which will be visibly manifested in the life of the church and will bear witness to the divine mission of Christ. To reach across denominational barriers, cultures, and those who know what the Spirit is saying to the church/body of Christ Jesus.

Leadership must come back to the basics of the Gospel of Jesus Christ and the ministry of the apostolic offices. The driving force to reach this result is to distinguish between the support, service, and sign gifts, and to compel believers to embrace God's apostolic order for the church. The gifts are given for a purpose. This discourse is not all inclusive but will show in the Bible where each gift is introduced, supported, and the application and use of each gift. The administration gifts are just as important as the foundational gifts, but are hardly given the credit they so well deserve.

DR ETHEL REID-SMITH

INTRODUCTION

A historical view is given concerning the church in Acts 2:37-41, lays out the intended apostolic order of God's church more than any other in the New Testament. It is evident that the Lord intended the church in Jerusalem, His church, be used as an example to other local churches throughout eternity. If you would take notice, the churches of the New Testament were named for their geographical locations. The authenticity of the Jerusalem church's existence is validated by the Lord's death, burial, resurrection, and ascension taking place in the capital and leading city which gave the world its Savior. The church began on the first Pentecost following the ascension of Jesus Christ. On the day of Pentecost the Holy Spirit fell upon the apostles, enabling them to preach the gospel, and 3000 were baptized and added to the church. For the first ten years, the church was comprised of Jewish Christians or Gentiles who had been proselytized into Judaism.

The Jerusalem church's strengths were; (a) brotherly love and unity, (b) immediate settlement of internal problems, (c) involvement of all of the members in the deliberations and resolutions of the problems that arose, (d) courage and devotion which led them to continue teaching even in the face of persecution, and (e) an excellent program of teaching which edified the disciples and gave the church such great teachers as Stephen, Philip, Barnabas, and Silas. The weaknesses of the Jerusalem church were; (a) poverty, (b) lying of Ananias and Sapphira, (c) neglect of the widows, (d) persecution, and (e) false teaching.

The difference between the apostolic order of the church that God intended and today's church is that the people of God are failing to recognize the difference between the authority of Jesus Christ, and carnality of the doctrine taught and the life styles lived by the present day leadership. Some leaders today are more than ever moving towards reconstructing their local churches according to their own doctrine and beliefs. Today there are other leaders reconstructing in the model of the intended apostolic order of God. These leaders are empowering their members and equipping them to do apostolic ministry according to Ephesians the 4th chapter. The apostolic order of God as illustrated by the Apostle Paul, describes the five-fold ministry; the apostle, prophet, evangelist, and pastor/teacher, and the way these gifts should operate in the church today. The five fold ministry offices and gifts can fully operate in the church only by the members being completely equipped or trained, mentored, and imparted into by the laying on of hands by the presbytery.

Training is the focus and purpose of these churches to ensure that those who are called do not operate illegally. Also, the leaders should be able to discern and recognize what gifting is embedded in those intended for leadership. The intended apostolic order of God does not consists or evolve into denominations, it is the correct way the church should function. First, God is spirit, and to comprehend the order of God it must be done by His Spirit. When God created man he breathed His breath into him and he became, God breathed Himself into us. It is reasonable to assume that God will lead and guide by His Spirit. Those who listen, hear, and obey His instructions will do the will of God for His church. Just as God gave Moses specific instructions to build His temple, He gave specific instructions for how He wants His church to be today.

Just as there is an order to creation, there is an order or structure to the church or body of Christ. The church does not exemplify God's apostolic order today. God has specific plans for the church that he gave to Christ his son, and Jesus gave them to the apostles. The church of the living God is Christ centered, loving, equipping, and concerned about the social atmosphere whether in the community or abroad. The founder and establisher of the church is Christ Jesus. The apostles continued the work of Christ by making disciples of every nation, spreading the Gospel, and empowering the people to carry on the work of Jesus Christ.

The church today has lost its focus and has become too commercialized and carnal. We have allowed erroneous doctrinal teachings, the traditions of men, and beliefs to divide, control and enslave the body as well as put denominations against one another. This is not what God intended the church to be, for God is not a God of confusion and chaos, God is a God of order, love and righteousness. The apostolic five fold ministry is that order along with the ministerial gifts. The church of today has all but excluded the offices of the apostle, prophet, evangelist, and teacher. After Jesus received his instructions from His Father, He said I do nothing of myself, but what the Father tells me. As believers and followers of Christ we have allowed our dogma and beliefs to supersede what God planned for his church. Jesus is the chief cornerstone, and the apostles built on the foundations of the teachings of Christ Jesus. We are to do exploits and greater works than Christ by teaching the Kingdom of God and His righteousness.

To get a better understanding of God's intended apostolic order for His church, an etymology of the word church itself will be explored as well as looking at the way it is used in context. This will be accomplished by tracing the church's earliest origins through Greek topical research of the matter.

TABLE OF CONTENTS

FOREWORD 5
PREFACE 7
MANDATE 9
INTRODUCTION 15

Chapter

1. THE DEFINITION OF CHURCH 21
   Ecclesia or Kyriakon
   The Old Testament
   The New Testament

2. THE ORIGINAL CHURCH 33
   The Early Church
   Church After the Ascension

3. PAULIAN VIEW 37
   Paul the Apostle
   Church's Mission

4. THE APOSTLES 45

5. APOSTOLIC ORDER 51
   Definition and purpose of the Five-Fold Ministry
   God's Apostolic Order Revealed

6. THE CHURCH'S STRUCTURE AND BEYOND 63
   Denominationalism
   God's Blueprint

7. THE NEW TESTAMENT CHURCH 73

8. THE FIVE-FOLD MINISTRY 83

9. THE CHURCH; THE BODY OF CHRIST 97

10. GOD'S PLAN FOR HIS CHURCH	109
11. COUNTERFEIT MINISTRY	117
12. GOD'S MANDATE FOR APOSTOLIC ORDER	129
13. KINGDOM APOSTOLIC ORDER I	137
14. SYSTEMATIC APOSTOLIC ORDER	151
15. KINGDOM APOSTOLIC ORDER II	165
BIBLIOGRAPHY………………………………………	177
SUGGESTIONS, QUESTIONS & THOUGHTS	179

CHAPTER I.
THE DEFINITION OF CHURCH

Ekklesia

As we examine the apostolic order that God mandated, we see how the word church is used in the Bible. Throughout the Scriptures church referred to people, never to a building. The Church (the Body of Christ) is made up of people called to follow Jesus Christ. The concept of people assembling to learn the teachings of God and His righteousness is embedded in the writings of the Old and New Testaments. Just as the children of Israel cried out to the God of their fathers, Abraham, Isaac, and Jacob; so do we the children of God cry out to His son, Jesus Christ for restoration of the church back to God's order with signs and wonders following.

The Greek word for church is *ekklesia*, which is simply the word for an "assembly" of citizens. In the Septuagint[1], the term was used for the general assembly of the Jewish people, especially when gathered for a religious purpose such as to listen to the Law (Deut. 9:10, 18:16). In the New Testament, the term *ekklesia* is used of the entire body of believers throughout the world. For instance, in Matthew 16:18, according to Scofield's commentary, the words, "thou art Peter [Greek, "petros" -- literally 'a little

---

[1] The Septuagint is the most ancient translation of the Old Testament and consequently is invaluable to critics for understanding and correcting the Hebrew text Massorah, the latter, such as it has come down to us, being the text established by the Massoretes in the sixth century A.D.

rock]', and upon this rock [Greek, "Petra"] I will build my church." He does not promise to build His church upon Peter, but upon Himself, as Peter is careful to tell us. It is also used of the believers in a particular area in Acts 5:11, talks about sin in the church, and for a group meeting in a particular house Romans 16:5, addresses how Aquilla was helpful in the administration of the church.

The Holman Bible Dictionary, in its article "Church," explains the background of the word church; "Church" is the English translation of the Greek word ekklesia. The use of the Greek term prior to the emergence of the Christian church is important as two streams of meaning flow from the history of its usage into the New Testament church. First, the Greek term which basically means "called out" was commonly used to indicate an assembly of citizens of a Greek city and is so used in Acts 19:32, 39. The citizens who were quite conscious of their privileged status over the slaves and noncitizens were called to the assembly and dealt with matters of common concern. When the early Christians understood themselves as constituting a church, they perceived themselves as called out. This was done by God through Jesus Christ for a special purpose and that their status became one in Jesus Christ (Ephesians 2:19).

Second, the Greek term was used more than one hundred times in the Greek translation of the Old Testament and was in common use in the time of Jesus. The Hebrew term qahal meant simply 'assembly' and could be used in a variety of ways. Referring for example to an assembling of prophets (1 Samuel 19:20), soldiers (Numbers 22:4), or the people of God (Deut. 9:10). The use of the term in the Old Testament in referring to the people of God is important for understanding the term 'church' in the New Testament.

The Wikipedia free internet encyclopedia defines the church as; a Christian Church is the universal institution embodying the Christian faith, the religion based on the worship of Jesus of Nazareth as the son of God. The concept as it was known beginning in 30-33 A.D., expresses the idea that the followers of the religion can all be seen as part of one single group.

The original Church was Apostolic in nature which means the church originated with the apostles, or having a direct link to the apostles. The three aspects of the apostolic according to Catholic teachings are; the church was planted in the world by the apostles, adheres to the teaching of the Jesus Christ, and carries on the succession of the apostolic ministry. This was a form of 'ecclesiola' it is not out to change the whole church, but to form a church within a church which would form a nucleus of true believers inside the general church. Their object in the formation of this nucleus was that it might act as a leaven and influence the life of the whole church for the better. It was not a movement, but something that was to happen in individual local churches. The opposite has occurred in the ecclesiola or ecclesia. Divisions, schisms, teaching of erroneous doctrine, self-imposed dogma, and self grandiose have infiltrated the body of Christ.

Thus, God's order for His church was established by Jesus Christ and implemented by the apostles with Jesus being the chief cornerstone has been distorted and skewed. Christ is not only the foundation of His church, but He is also its architect and builder. The church is a holy temple, a habitation of God, through the Holy Spirit who indwells every born-again child of God (1 Corinthians 6:19, 20). Jesus Christ built His church on the doctrine of the apostles and prophets, and He is the foundation and chief cornerstone of His church. What has in the church occurred today, is the teachings of the apostles have been distorted and changed to reflect the beliefs of carnal men. These erroneous teachings were created to manipulate and control the body of Christ.

The Catholic Church fathers has been such as; translated the early church writings to reflect their opinions and beliefs. Some were not Spirit filled and their writings allowed for human error which has led to the misrepresentation of God's original apostolic order, and the teaching of Christ and His disciples. They also relegated the Baptism in the Holy Ghost, and the laying on of hands only to the presbytery. After Judas Ischariot committed suicide from the guilt of His betrayal of Christ, another apostle was chosen. The eleven apostles went into prayer to consult God for the apostle He chose to replace Judas (Acts 1:21-24). I am convinced that if the early church fathers were Spirit filled and consulted the Father for His inspiration, there would be less schism and separation within the body of Christ.

Ekklesia or Kyriakon

The Old Testament or Septuagint meaning of church

In order to understand the complete origin of the meaning of church, first, lets take a look at the Septuagint translators of the Old Testament. Although in one or two places (Psalm 25:5; Judith 6:21; etc.) the word is used without religious signification, merely in the sense of "an assembly", this is not usually the case. Ordinarily it is employed as the Greek equivalent of the Hebrew *qahal*, i.e., the entire community of the children of Israel viewed in their religious aspect. Two Hebrew words are employed in the Old Testament to signify the congregation of Israel, viz. *qahal 'êdah*.

The Septuagint renders church as, respectively, *ekklesia* and *synagoge*. Thus in Proverbs, where the words occur together, "in the midst of the church and the congregation", the Greek rendering is *en meso ekklesias kai synagoges*. The distinction is indeed not rigidly observed -- thus in Exodus, Leviticus and Numbers, both words are regularly represented by *synagogue*. It is adhered to in the great majority of cases, and may be regarded as an established rule. In the writings of the New Testament the words are sharply distinguished. With them *ecclesia* denotes the Church of Christ; *synagoga*, the Jews still adhering to the worship of the Old Covenant. Occasionally, it is true, *ecclesia* is employed in its general significance of "assembly" (Acts 19:32; 1 Corinthians 14:19); and *synagoga* occurs once in reference to a gathering of Christians, though apparently of a non-religious character (James 2:2). But *ecclesia* is never used by the Apostles to denote the Jewish Church. The word as a technical expression had been transferred to the community of Christian believers. It is interesting to note that the Septuagint, third century B. C. Greek translation of the Hebrew Scriptures, uses ekklesia throughout the Old Testament Scriptures to describe the assembly of the people of Israel.

God gave Moses specific instructions on how to construct the temple with the outer court symbolizing the body, the inner court representing the soul, and the inner court the Spirit of God. The temple later was used symbolically for the human body, and the dwelling place of God. During creation every thing created was dependent on the proceeding day for existence. For example, the water had to be separated from the firmament for the creation of seas, and bodies of water for the habitation and existence of sea creatures. The seventh day or the Sabbath was set aside for God.

The first mention of order was in Deuteronomy when God gave specific instructions to Moses for the order in which the temple was to be built. The Hebrew name for tabernacle is "Mishkan, or sanctuary a dwelling place for God". The metaphor used in the New Testament for tabernacle is temple which refers to the body as a sanctuary for God's dwelling. The presence of the Spirit in the Church is the presence of the Lord: "the Lord is the Spirit. Thus the "one body" which the one Spirit created is the Body of Christ. To be in the Spirit is to be in Christ.

The New Testament meaning of church

The English term "church" is supposed to be a derivative of the Greek term kuriakos, meaning "of or belonging to the Lord." It is used to translate the Greek term *ekklesia,* which occurs 115 times in the New Testament, with all but four occurrences (Acts 7:38; 19:32,39,41) referring to God's people of the new covenant. *Ekklesia* is a compound formed from the Greek preposition ek (meaning "out of" and the Greek noun klesis (meaning "a calling"). Hence, the "church" is literally "that which is called out of the realm of sin and darkness into the light and kingdom of Jesus Christ (Col. 1:13; II Thess. 2:14).

It is noteworthy that Jesus used the term "church" only three times in two different passages, but His usage of the term illustrates the two basic senses in which it is used in the New Testament. When He said, "I will build My church" (Matt. 16:18), He used the term in the *universal* sense, including all of His disciples throughout the world. When He said that differences between brethren should ultimately be taken to the church (Matt. 18:15-17), He used the term in the local sense, referring to a body of His disciples within a particular geographical area who band together for purposes of work and worship. Sometimes modifying phrases (I Cor. 1:2; Rom. 16:16), or different terms (I Cor. 3:16; Eph. 1:22, 23; Col. 1:13), are used in reference to the church to emphasize different aspects of it.

Jesus Christ is the designer, architect and builder of the church, for He said "I will build My church" (Matt. 16:18). For this reason it bears His name (Rom. 16:16). No church which was founded by men or bears the name of a man (as well as humanly devised names) can have been the church founded by Christ. Eph 2:20 the church is compared to a building. The apostles and prophets are *the foundation* of that building. They may be so called in a secondary sense, Christ himself being the primary foundation; but we are rather to understand it of the doctrine delivered by the prophets of the Old Testament and the apostles of the New. It follows, *Jesus Christ himself being the chief corner-stone.* In him both Jews and Gentiles meet, and constitute one church; and Christ supports the building by his strength: *In whom all the building, fitly framed together,* etc., Eph 2:21. All believers, of whom it consists, being united to Christ by faith, and among themselves by Christian charity, *grow unto a holy temple,* become a sacred society, in which there is much communion between God and his people, as in the temple, they worshipping and serving him, he manifesting himself unto them, they offering up spiritual sacrifices to God and he dispensing his blessings and favors to them. Thus the building, for the nature of it, is a temple, a holy temple; for the church is the place which God hath chosen to put his name there, and it becomes such a temple by grace and strength derived from himself - *in the Lord.* The universal church being built upon Christ as the foundation-stone, and united in Christ as the corner-stone, comes at length to be glorified in him as the top-stone: *In whom you also are built together,* etc., Eph 2:22. Observe, Not only the universal church is called the temple of God, but particular churches; and even every true believer is a living temple, is *a habitation of God through the Spirit.* God dwells in all believers now, they having become the temple of God through the operations of the blessed Spirit, and his dwelling with them now is an earnest of their dwelling together with him to eternity.[2]

---

[2] Matthew Henry Commentary

The foundation of the church is *Jesus Christ in His divine nature as the Son of God* (Matt. 16:16; I Cor. 3:11). There is no stronger or surer foundation on which the church may be built, and any church which is established upon a different principle does not have that distinctive, essential feature which marks it as a true church of Christ.

The city of *Jerusalem* is obviously the place where the church of Christ began. Old Testament prophecies pointed to Jerusalem as the place where God would establish His house, the church (Isa. 2:2,3). Jesus specified Jerusalem as the "beginning" place for the preaching of repentance (Lk. 24:47), and He told His apostles to remain there until the coming of the Holy Spirit (Lk. 24:49; Acts 1:4,5). It was in Jerusalem that the Holy Spirit came upon the apostles, the gospel was preached, and men were baptized and added to the church (Acts 2). As a matter of fact, for the first seven chapters of Acts the church is never mentioned as existing anywhere but in Jerusalem and its environs (Acts 2:47; 5:11).

It is also quite evident that the church began on the first *Pentecost* following Jesus' ascension. Prior to Pentecost the church is spoken of as being in the future (Matt. 16:18), and after Pentecost it is spoken of as being then in existence (Acts 2:47; 5:11; 8:1). This agrees with the fact that the gospel, which saves men and obedience to which grants church membership, was first preached in its fullness on the day of Pentecost. Is it any wonder, then, that Peter later refers to the events of Pentecost as "the beginning" (Acts 11 :15).

The New Testament writers used the Greek term ekklesia and it was their version of the Hebrew Scriptures and was common for them to use. The word church came from a Greek word meaning of the Lord or kyriakon. The earliest record of kyriakon was approximately two hundred years after Jesus and the twelve apostles died. In William E. Vine's dictionary of New Testament Words, there is no mention of the Greek word for church. Instead for church there is reference to assembly and congregation. The reason he does not mention a Greek word for church is the early church writings did not have a Greek word for church.

The origins of the English word for church according to Merriam Webster Online Dictionary, comes from Middle English chirche, from Old English cirice, from Late Greek kyriakon, from

Greek, neutor of kyriakos of the Lord, and from kyrios Lord, master. In the Blue Letter Bible Dictionary and Word Search the Greek word kuriakos from which the English word for church is derived. Kuriakos is in the New Testament only twice and translates once as the Lord's supper, and once as the Lord's day, but not as church. The Greek root English word church isn't used in the New Testament as church, its not there.

In researching to find out how the word church originated, The King James Bible – A Brief History, concludes that King James established rules to govern the work of translating the Bible. One was that Ecclesiastical words such as church and priest were to be used to translate their Greek counterparts. King James controlled the Anglican church and the common people.

There is no etymological syntax between the Greek word kyriakon and the Greek term ekklesia, they are entirely two different words. Words like church or churches do not convey the meaning of the Greek term ekklesia. The Online Etymology Dictionary confirms the Greek work kyriakos as the origin of the English word church, but is also states that kyriakos was used for houses of Christian worship since c. 300. Therefore, the correct Greek translation for kyriakos is the building, and ekkclesia is the people.

Jesus stated in Matthew 16:18 that he was going to build his ekklesia or as the 1898 Young's Literal Translation states, "I will build my assembly. . .". The rendering removes all the preconceived assumptions and religious connotations that the word church has and makes it clear that Jesus is talking about his people. Another example is found in I Timothy 3:15 in the phrase, "the house of God, which is the church of the living God. . ." . The Greek reads; oikos, theos hostis esti ekklesia zao theos. Meaning, "the house [oikos {oy-kos}] of God, which is the assembly of the called out people [ekklesia {ek-klay-see'ah}] of the living God. God dwells within his people individually and collectively, not in buildings called churches. We are the assembly of the called out ones of God that make up a living house of the living God.

Now, therefore, God's intended apostolic order for His church is built on the foundation of the apostles, prophets and Jesus Christ being the chief cornerstone, in whom the whole building, being fitted together, grows into a holy temple in the Lord, in whom you are being built together for a dwelling place of God in the Spirit. (Ephesians 2:19-20). The church is not a building, but an assembly of people. People are the church.

The following shows the development of the word church in its various word forms, tracing back to the Greek kyriaka, the plural form of kyriakon.

- 1600 – church becomes the common spelling during the long process of standardization.
- 1500 – church, churche, chirch, chirche, chyrch, chyrche, church, cherche
- 1400 – churche, chirch, chirche, chyrch, chyrche, cherch, cherche
- 1300 – churche, chirch, chirche, chyrch, chyrche, cherch, cheche
- 1200 – churche, chureche, churiche, cherche, chereche, chyrche
- 1100 – chirche, chiriche, chireche, chyreche, chyrce (Middle English period 1100- 1500)
- 1000 – cirice, cyrice, circe, cyrce (Old English/Anglo-Saxon period 600-1100)
- 300+ - kirika, kerika (W. German/Old Saxon – Pre-English period)
- 200+ - kyriaka/kuriaka, the plural form of kyriakon (Greek)

However, linguists may differ on the exact development of the word church. Most agree it comes from the Greek kyriakon, belonging to the Lord, and its uses dates back to the third century.

CHAPTER II.
THE ORIGINAL CHURCH

Ekklesia or Kyriakon

The Early Church

The Old Testament or Septuagint meaning of church

In order to understand the complete origin of the meaning of church, first, lets take a look at the Septuagint translators of the Old Testament. Although in one or two places (Psalm 25:5; Judith 6:21; etc.) the word is used without religious signification, merely in the sense of "an assembly", this is not usually the case. Ordinarily it is employed as the Greek equivalent of the Hebrew *qahal*, i.e., the entire community of the children of Israel viewed in their religious aspect. Two Hebrew words are employed in the Old Testament to signify the congregation of Israel, viz. *qahal 'êdah*.

The Septuagint renders church as, respectively, *ekklesia* and *synagoge*. Thus in Proverbs, where the words occur together, "in the midst of the church and the congregation", the Greek rendering is *en meso ekklesias kai synagoges*. The distinction is indeed not rigidly observed -- thus in Exodus, Leviticus and Numbers, both words are regularly represented by *synagogue*. It is adhered to in the great majority of cases, and may be regarded as an established rule. In the writings of the New Testament the words are sharply distinguished. With them *ecclesia* denotes the

Church of Christ; *synagoga*, the Jews still adhering to the worship of the Old Covenant. Occasionally, it is true, *ecclesia* is employed in its general significance of "assembly" (Acts 19:32; 1 Corinthians 14:19); and *synagoga* occurs once in reference to a gathering of Christians, though apparently of a non-religious character (James 2:2). But *ecclesia* is never used by the Apostles to denote the Jewish Church. The word as a technical expression had been transferred to the community of Christian believers. It is interesting to note that the Septuagint, third century B. C. Greek translation of the Hebrew Scriptures, uses ekklesia throughout the Old Testament Scriptures to describe the assembly of the people of Israel.

The New Testament meaning of church

Gods intended apostolic order for the church today has emasculated into a perverse version of church order. The original church was established in Jerusalem and Israel through; commissioning, apostolic empowerment, witnessing, serving, persecution, deliverance from legalists, and by strengthening. Soon after Christ ascension, He commanded that everyone be evangelized in Jerusalem, Samaria, and among all nations. The early church had all in things common so there was not anything lacking among the believers. In one or two places of the Septuagint translations of the Old Testament in Psalm 25:5 and Judith 6:21, the word ecclesia is used without religious significance and is used in the sense of an assembly.

Jesus Christ founded the original church and established the master-disciple relationship of the apostolic order God intended. This church was a spiritually transformed body of believers. The first place we find the word church is in Matthew 16:18 where Jesus is speaking to Peter. The Greek word ekklesia translated here as church appears 115 places in the New Testament and is also translated as assembly or congregation.

The original church spans or New Testament church spans a period of twenty to thirty years. This church was established in 30 A. D. Between the time of His resurrection and the founding of His church, Christ appeared to His apostles for 40 days, further enlightening them concerning the nature of the Kingdom of God (Acts 1:3). During this time, "He commanded them not to depart from Jerusalem, but to wait for the Promise of the Father" (Acts 1: 4). He explained to them: " ...You shall receive power when the Holy Ghost has come upon you; and you shall be witnesses to Me in Jerusalem, and in all Judea and Samaria, and to the end of the earth" (Acts 1: 8).

The Church after the Ascension

The doctrine of the Church as set forth by the Apostles after the Ascension of Christ Jesus, is identical with the teaching of Christ just described. Peter, in his first sermon, delivered on the day of Pentecost, declares that Jesus of Nazareth is the Messiah (Acts 2:36). The means of salvation which he indicates is baptism; and by baptism his converts are aggregated to disciples. In these days the Christians still availed themselves of the Temple services. The tie of unity was so close that it brought about in the Church of Jerusalem the condition of all things in which the disciples had all things common.

Christ had declared that His kingdom should be spread among all nations, and had committed the execution of the work to the twelve apostles (Matthew 28:19). Yet the universal mission of the Church revealed itself gradually. Peter makes mention of it in (Acts 2:39). But in the earliest years apostolic activity is confined to Jerusalem alone. Indeed an old tradition. The first notable advance occurs on the persecution which arose after the death of Stephen, A. D. 37. This was the occasion of preaching of the Gospel to the Samaritans, a people excluded from the privileges of Israel, though acknowledging the Mosaic Law (Acts 8:5). A still further expansion resulted from the revelation directing Peter to admit to baptizing Cornelius, a devout Gentile, i.e. one associated to the Jewish religion but not circumcised. more than fifteen years after Christ's Ascension when, at Antioch in Pisidia, Paul and Barnabas announced that since the Jews accounted themselves unworthy of eternal life they would "turn to the Gentiles".

In the Apostolic teaching the term *Church*, from the very first, takes the place of the expression *Kingdom of God* (Acts

5:11). Where others than the Jews were concerned, the greater suitability of the former name is evident; for *Kingdom of God* had special reference to Jewish beliefs. But the change of title only emphasizes the social unity of the members. They are the new congregation of Israel -- the theocratic polity: they are the people (*laos*) of God (Acts 15:14; Romans 9:25; 2 Corinthians 6:16; 1 Peter 2:9 sq.; Hebrews 8:10; Revelation 18:4; 21:3). By their admission to the Church, the Gentiles have been grafted in and form part of God's fruitful olive-tree, while apostate Israel has been broken off (Romans 11:24). Paul writing to his Gentile converts at Corinth, terms the ancient Hebrew Church "our fathers" (1 Corinthians 10:1). Indeed from time to time the previous phraseology is employed, and the Gospel message is termed the preaching of the Kingdom of God (Acts 20:25; 28:31).

Within the Church the Apostles exercised that regulative power with which Christ had endowed them. It was no chaotic mob, but a true society possessed of a corporate life, and organized in various orders. The evidence shows that the twelve possessed (a) a power of jurisdiction, in virtue of which they wielded a legislative and judicial authority, and (b) a magisterial office to teach the Divine revelation entrusted to them. Thus (a) we find Paul authoritatively prescribing for apostolic order and practices of the churches. He does not advise; he directs (1 Corinthians 11:34; 26:1; Titus 1:5). He pronounces judicial sentence (1 Corinthians 5:5; 2 Corinthians 2:10), and his sentences, like those of other Apostles, receive at times the solemn sanction of miraculous punishment (1 Timothy 1:20; Acts 5:1-10).

In like manner he bids his delegate Timothy to hear the causes even of priests, and rebuke, in the sight of all, those who sin (1 Timothy 5:19 sq.). (b) With no less definiteness does he assert that the Apostolate carries with it a doctrinal authority, which all are bound to recognize. God has sent them to establish His order, he affirms them, to claim "the obedience of faith" (Romans 1:5; 15:18). Further, his solemnly expressed desire, that even if an angel from heaven were to preach another doctrine to the Galatians than that which he had delivered to them, he should be anathema (Galatians 1:8), involves a claim to infallibility in the teaching of revealed truth.

The origins of the Orthodox Church can be traced back continuously to the earliest Christian movement. So can the Roman Catholic Church, the Anglican Community, and many other Christian faith groups. Each has their own belief system about their group's origins. The following is based on the historical record, rather than on any one group's beliefs.

CHAPTER III.
PAULINIAN VIEW

Circa 30 CE: Founding of Christianity:

Christianity was founded by Yeshua of Nazareth, now generally referred to as Jesus Christ , a Greek translation of Yeshua, Messiah. After preaching mostly in Judea for three years (according to the Gospel of John) or mostly in the Galilee for one year (according to the other three canonical gospels) he traveled to Jerusalem just before Passover. After having committed aggravated assault in the Temple he was convicted of treason or insurrection in Palestine by the Roman occupying forces. Yeshua was executed there, sometime in the late 20's or early 30's CE.

His followers formed the *Jewish Christian* movement under the leadership of James, the brother of Jesus. (The term "brother" in this context has been interpreted by the Orthodox Church as referring to one of Jesus' step-brothers fathered by Joseph in a previous marriage.)[3] They viewed themselves as a reform movement within Judaism. They organized a synagogue, worshiped and brought animals for ritual sacrifice at the Jerusalem Temple. They viewed Jesus as a prophet and rabbi, but not as a

---

[3] *"Did Jesus have brothers?"* at:
http://www.rockinauburn.com/columns/

deity. They observed the Jewish holy days, practiced circumcision of their male children, followed kosher dietary laws, and practiced the teachings of Jesus as they interpreted them to be. Many were killed, enslaved, or scattered during the Roman attack on Jerusalem in 70 CE. The movement struggled on for many decades, but eventually disappeared.

Circa 36 CE: Pauline Christianity:

Paul was born at Tarsus in Cilicia (Acts 21:39), of a father who was a Roman citizen (Acts 22:26-28; cf. 16:37), of a family in which piety was hereditary (2 Timothy 1:3) and who was attached to Pharisaic traditions and observances (Philippians 3:5-6).
His parents were natives of Gischala, a small town of Galilee and that they brought him to Tarsus when Gischala was captured by the Romans. Paul received a revelation of God's order of His church as laid out in Ephesians the 4th chapter.

He belonged to the tribe of Benjamin he was given at the time of his circumcision the name of Saul, which must have been common in that tribe in memory of the first king of the Jews (Philippians 3:5). As a Roman citizen he also bore the Latin name of Paul. It was quite usual for the Jews of that time to have two names, one Hebrew, the other Latin or Greek, between which there was often a certain assonance and which were joined together exactly in the manner made use of by Luke (Acts 13:9: *Saulos ho kai Paulos*).

Every respectable Jew had to teach his son a trade, young Saul learned how to make tents (Acts 18:3) or rather to make the mohair of which tents were made (cf. Lewin, "Life of St. Paul", I, London, 1874, 8-9). He was still very young when sent to Jerusalem to receive his education at the school of Gamaliel (Acts 22:3). Possibly some of his family resided in the holy city; later there is mention of the presence of one of his sisters whose son saved his life (Acts 23:16).

From that time it was impossible to follow him until he takes an active part in the martyrdom of St. Stephen (Acts 7:58-60;

22:20). He was then qualified as a young man (*neanias*), but this might be applied to a man between twenty and forty.

Saul, a Jew from Tarsus, experienced a powerful religious conversion on the road to Damascus, Syria. Later, as Paul, he became the single most important Christian leader from about 36 CE until his execution in the mid-60's.

Paul went on a series of missionary journeys which prepared him to establish churches around the eastern Mediterranean in what is now Orthodox Church territory. He attracted many Gentiles (non-Jews) to his movement. Paul organized churches in many of the areas' urban centers. He and his movement were in continual theological conflict with the Jewish Christian movement centered in Jerusalem because he taught church order accordin to the Will of God. Paul ran afoul of Roman law, was arrested, and was transported to Rome where he was held under house arrest. He was executed there about 65 CE. Paul's churches survived his death and flourished.

Christian groups typically met in the homes of individual believers, much like home churches do today, but they followed the teachings of Paul. There was no central authority, no standard style of organization at the local level, no dedicated church buildings or cathedrals. The Greek words episkopos (bishop, overseer), presbuteros (elder, presbyter) and poimen (pastor, shepherd) were originally synonymous terms which referred simply to the leader of a group of believers.[4] The Hebrew Scriptures (Old Testament) was their holy book; the Christian Scriptures (New Testament) had not been assembled. By the time that Jesus' original followers (now called Apostles) died, most of the Christians in the world were Gentiles following Pauline Christianity.

Another competitor to Pauline Christianity was Gnostic Christianity, a philosophical and religious movement with roots in pre-Christian times. Gnostics combined elements taken from

---

[4] *Constantine, the first Christian emperor,*" Antiquity Online, at: http://www.fsmitha.com/h1/ch24.htm

Asian, Babylonian, Egyptian, Greek and Syrian pagan religions, from astrology, and from Judaism and Christianity. They claimed to have secret knowledge about God, humanity, and the rest of the universe of which the general population was unaware. They believed that the Jehovah of the Hebrew Scriptures was a defective, inferior Creator-God, also known as *the Demiurge*. He was viewed as fundamentally evil, jealous, rigid, lacking in compassion and prone to committing genocide. They viewed Jesus as a deity in human form, but not a human. They tolerated different religious beliefs within and outside of Gnosticism. Some Gnostics formed separate congregations; others joined existing Pauline Christian groups; still others were solitary practitioners.

Second and third centuries CE:

Pauline Christianity continued to spread across the known world. It started to develop a formal theology, a set of doctrines, and an unofficial canon of writings which were later to become the Christian Scriptures. Much of this development of dogma was in response to frictions between the Pauline and Gnostic branches of the early Christian movement. The *Apostolic Fathers or Roman Popes,* had replaced the original apostles by this time.

They included a number of teachers and bishops: e.g. Clement of Alexandria, Irenaeus, Origen, Polycarp, Tertullian. A hierarchical organizational structure called the "*monarchial episcopate*" developed in which the individual congregational leaders recognized the authority of their area bishop in matters of doctrine and faith. There was considerable friction between the Christian movement and the Roman Empire. Christians were viewed as Atheists because they did not believe in multiple gods and goddesses. They were viewed as irresponsible citizens because many refused to sacrifice in the Pagan temples. Christians came under intermittent and serious oppression.

Fourth century CE:

The years of Christian persecution came to an end in 313 CE. Emperor Constantine (289-337 CE) issued the *Edict of Milan* which formally established freedom and toleration for Christianity. Jews lost many rights with this edict. There was no single individual who spoke for all of Christianity. The only way in which the Church could resolve matters of belief and practice was to have all of the bishops assemble at a council to debate and vote. The first such meeting was the *Council of Nicea,* held in Asia Minor (now Turkey) during 325 CE. Only 318 bishops out of the approximately 1,800 Christian bishops then in existence attended. Most came from the Eastern half of the Roman Empire.[5] Much of the debate at this and subsequent councils dealt with the precise nature of Jesus and his relationship to Jehovah and the Holy Spirit.

Circa 330 CE

Emperor Constantine decided to build a "*New Rome*" on the site of the Greek city of Byzantium (now at Istanbul, Turkey). It was called Constantinople. It became the center of the largely Christian empire. ₂ By this time, the church had evolved from a small, scattering of congregations to a geographically widespread church under the authority of many bishops.

Later in the fourth century, Emperor Theodosian issued a series of decrees or rescripts to "*suppress all rival religions, order the closing of the temples, and impose fines, confiscation, imprisonment or death upon any who cling to the older [Pagan] religions.*" [6] The period of relative religious tolerance under Paganism in the Roman Empire ended as non-Christian temples were seized and converted to Christian use or destroyed. Priests

---

[5] *Constantine, the first Christian emperor,*" Antiquity Online, at: http://www.fsmitha.com/h1/ch24.htm

[6] Joseph McCabe, "*A Rationalist Encyclopaedia: A book of reference on religion, philosophy, ethics and science,*" Gryphon Books (1971). Excerpts appear at: http://www.christianism.com/articles/18.html

and Priestesses were exiled or killed. Pauline Christianity and Judaism were the only permitted religions. To follow another faith group was an offense punishable by death.

Church authority became concentrated in the five bishops or patriarchs located in Alexandria, Antioch, Constantinople, Jerusalem and Rome. At the ecumenical council of 381, Rome was given the lead position, followed by Constantinople and then Alexandria. Their ranking followed the secular status of the bishops' cities in the Roman Empire. Each of the five patriarchs was totally sovereign within his sphere of jurisdiction. [5]

Fifth Century CE:

In 451 CE, the *Council of Chalcedon* was called to resolve still another debate about Jesus. The *East Syrian* (Nestorian) church and the *Oriental Orthodox Christian Church* disagreed with the council's decision that Christ had two natures, one human and one divine. They split off from the rest of Christianity in the first major schism from Pauline Christianity. Also during the 5th century, various Germanic tribes invaded Rome and destroyed much of the Western Roman Empire. The church centered in Rome successfully converted the invaders to Christianity. Authority within the church began to coalesce around the Bishop of Rome in the west and the Patriarch of Constantinople in the east. Divisions between the two power centers in the Christian church gradually intensified.

Sixth century CE:

Emperor Justinian called The *Second Council of Constantinople* for 533 CE. He invited equal numbers of bishops from each of the five patriarchal sees: Alexandria, Antioch, Constantinople, Jerusalem and Rome. The Bishop of Rome at the time, Pope Vigilius, saw that many more bishops from the east than from the west would be present; he refused to attend. *While the intellectual thought of Eastern Christianity was driven by Greek teachers, Western Christianity came to be dominated by the teachings of Augustine of Hippo."* (354 - 386 CE). *Although the two regions belonged to the same church, they became increasingly remote from each other."* [7]

The formal split did not occur until 1054 CE when the leaders of the Roman Catholic Church and Eastern Orthodox churches excommunicated each other.

---

[7] David Levinson, "*Religion: A cross cultural dictionary,*" Oxford University Press, (1996). Topics: Eastern Orthodoxy & Roman Catholicism.

DR ETHEL REID-SMITH

CHAPTER IV.
THE APOSTLES

Each Apostle had a proclivity to act out his own personality, but being individuals they still chose to teach the same Gospel in various ways and various demographics. There are three aspects of the "apostolic" the church was planted in the world by the apostles, and we are to adhere to the teaching of Jesus Christ. (H. B. Swete, Cambridge Regius, 1890-1915)
Christ did not intend for the believers to identify, follow the teachings of, or make a distinction between the teachings of Peter versus Paul.

The coming of the Holy Spirit on the Day of Pentecost (Acts 2:1-4) transformed the apostles of Jesus Christ from a group of ordinary men into some of the most remarkable and dynamic leaders the world has known. To appreciate the magnitude of their transformation, we need to take a close look at the same men before they received God's Spirit.

The four Gospels, Matthew, Mark, Luke and John, provide us with insight into their lives. We see no indication that the twelve apostles had an exceptional education or any position of influence. They were common men, regarded as uneducated and untrained by the rulers and religious authorities of that time (Acts 4:13).

Matthew was a tax collector, a member of one of the despised professions of his day (Matthew 9:9; 18:17). Peter, his brother Andrew and two other brothers James and John, were partners in a modes fishing enterprise (Matthew 4:18-22, Luke 5:1-

10). Along with Philip, they lived in the town of Bethsaida in the northern province of Galilee (John 1:44). The only special thing about them was that they were disciples, students and follower of Christ Jesus.

Another interesting fact about the apostles was the level of their lack of spiritual comprehension during their time of training. Their minds were still controlled by their fleshly nature, and their thinking and behavior were considered carnal (Romans 8:5-7). Jesus rebuked them for their lack of belief and hardness of heart (Mark 16:14). Their attitudes and behavior during that time illustrate that even living in the presence of Jesus Christ while He was on earth, personally hearing Him teach and seeing His example, was not sufficient to transform their thinking from carnal to spiritual.

Jesus sternly chastised James and John for their attitude toward some who had rejected Jesus. "But they (the Samaritans) did not receive Him …And when His disciples James and John saw this, they said, 'Lord, do You want us to command fire to come down from heaven and consume them, just as Elijah did?' But He turned and rebuked them, and said, 'You do not know what manner of spirit you are of; For the Son of Man did not come to destroy men's lives but to save them'" (Luke 9:53-57). John would later become known as the apostle of love which was quite a turn around for a man who had urged Jesus Christ to annihilate a village.

The disciples were selfish and contentious. They argued among themselves as to who would be the greatest (Mark 9:33-34; Luke 22:24). James and John even tried to finagle Jesus into awarding them the two most prominent positions in His Kingdom (Mark 10:35-37). Like many other people, each of them greatly overestimated his faithfulness and loyalty to Christ. Jesus said to them, "all of you will be made to stumble because of Me this night, for it is written: I will strike the Shepherd, and the sheep will be scattered" …Peter said to Him, even if all are made to stumble, yet I will not be. Jesus said to him, Assuredly, I say to that today, even this night, before the rooster crows twice, you will deny Me three times.' But he spoke more vehemently, 'If I have to die with

You, I will not deny You! And they all said likewise" (Mark 14:27-31).

As they spoke those words, the disciples believed they would loyally do as they had said. Yet, within hours they all abandoned Jesus to suffer alone (Mark 14:50). Peter even cursed and swore that he had never even known Jesus (Matthew 26:69-75; Luke 22:54-62). After Jesus execution, Peter and six of the other apostles decided it was time to give up all they had learned and resume their career as fishermen (John 21:2-3). They had heard Jesus speak about His death and resurrection, but they limited perspective blinded them to the significance of Jesus' sayings. That same blindness is a part of all human beings until God opens their understanding to see what He really says in His Word. Even after hearing reports of Jesus' resurrection, Thomas was so skeptical that he commented, "Unless I see in His hands the print of the nails, and put my finger into His side, I will not believe" (John 20:25). Jesus later appeared and provided Thomas with the precise proof he requested (verses 26-29).

These were the men Jesus chose to carry His gospel to every nation. As yet they had not received God's Spirit. They were as powerless as any other human would be to fulfill their commitment to faithfully serve their Savior. It was impossible for them to be the special servants of Christ on their own strength. Now we understand Jesus' remark when His disciples asked Him, "Who then can be saved?" His answer: "With men this is impossible, but with God all things are possible" (Matthew 19:25-26).

The leading characteristic of each apostle were:

Peter was impulsive; Andrew open-minded; James fanatical; John passionate; Philip inquisitive; Bartholomew composed; Matthew humble; Thomas pessimistic; James the son of Alphaeus quiet; Simon the Zealot strong-willed; Judas son of James intense; and Judas traitor.

Paul was the apostle to the Gentiles. It was his province, his area of rule, his area of influence. Paul was saying that he lived with it. He worked within it. He did not go into other men's areas to extend his influence beyond what was given to him. Peter was made first preeminent over them all and then as the work grew, God divided it up. He said, *"Paul you concentrate on this. Peter you concentrate on that."* They had the leadership in those areas and it was almost like the two shall never meet.

Paul adhered to the sphere of influence that God had given him, but so did the other twelve. They divided up the world, went to their area, and conducted their governmental responsibilities within that area. That was the only way that God could keep order. And the people in those areas who were responding to the teaching of those men were not confused by other voices speaking to them. Each stayed in his own sphere of influence, the one that had been given to them by God. And within that area, they were the top authority. God was able to keep order and the apostles were all speaking the same thing. The people were not confused and knew who were in their area for authorities in these matters pertaining to the order of God.

God is not the author of confusion. Doctrine was put into the church as the apostolic order that God intended as He did through Moses through whom He gave the first five books, as He did through Samuel who may very well have been the author all the way from Joshua up until the end of II Samuel, and then others whom God used to add to the scriptures so that we might have the complete Bible today.

The mandate of *Gods apostolic order is to* teach His doctrine and it should be taught by the man *or woman He chooses* to be His ambassador (His representative) to those who have been called. That keeps things in order we have to have faith in that, and in the pattern that God has ordained.

Apostolic order refers to the relationship between the Christian church today and the apostolic church of New Testament times. Thus, apostolic order refers to the whole church insofar as it is faithful to the Word and teachings of Jesus Christ, the witness, and the service of the apostolic communities. Understood in this way, the church is not simply a collective of individual churches; instead, it is a communion of churches whose validity is derived from the apostolic message that it professes and from the apostolic order that God intended.

Those who accept apostolic order as necessary for a valid ministry argue that it was necessary for Christ to establish a ministry to carry out his work and that he commissioned his

Apostles to do this (Matthew 28:19–20). The Apostles in turn consecrated and empowered others to assist them and to carry on the work. Supporters of the doctrine also argue that evidence indicates that the doctrine was accepted in the very early church. But, the apostolic order mandated by God was lost in the reinterpretation of the Gospels by the early Church Fathers when they rejected the apostolic revelation of Paul and the five ministry gifts.

The oneness Christ requests is not an organizational but a spiritual unity, which will be visibly manifested in the life of the church and will bear witness to the divine mission of Christ. To reach across denominational barriers, cultures, and those who know what the Spirit is saying to the church/body of Christ Jesus. Leadership must come back to the basics of the Gospel of Jesus Christ and the ministry of the apostolic offices. The driving force to reach this result is to distinguish between the support, service, and sign gifts, and to compel believers to embrace God's apostolic order for the church.

The Body of Christ must take into consideration that change is eminent, evident, and definite. We must embrace change or ultimately be left behind. It is absolute that God won't change but his strategies are innovative and unique. We have allowed others design what the church should be and do by excepting erroneous and ungodly doctrines and rituals. God's intended order is for the church to create His order as it is in Heaven on earth, by using His Word as our compass and law.

DR ETHEL REID-SMITH

CHAPTER V.
APOSTOLIC ORDER

The apostolic order of the church was revealed to Paul and the other apostles by the Holy Spirit. Paul describes the Church as a living organism, i.e. the body of Christ. This is to say that the Church is a "body" only with reference to the person of Christ. The first instance in which Paul works out this image of the body, with reference to the Church is 1Cor. 12;12-27 where he concludes in (v.27) that Christians form a body as members of it only because they are members of Christ by their appropriation of his saving work of themselves. In other words, the believers of Christ who are in Christ are members of the body because they received Christ as their Lord and savior and became a part of the body of Christ which is the Church.

Gentiles and Jews would form this one holy, redeemed body in Christ was not explicitly revealed through Old Testament prophets; only the New Testament prophets understood this truth. (John 10:16). Christ said that He would build His church upon Peters' confession that Jesus is "the Christ", the Messiah (Matthew 16:16-18). The church was composed both of believing Jews and Gentiles. The Gentiles of Old Testament days were strangers and foreigners –now they are fellow citizens and family members of the household of faith of God.

The church was planned to function as a harmonious temple structure, all parts being fitted together (Ephesians 2:21). This was an echo of Christ's command to the church, that you love one another (John 13:34, 35). Those who unlovingly disturb the fellowship and unity of the body, abuse and disobey the order of God for His church. The church was eternally planned and ordered by God to function according to Ephesians 4:11-16. Since the beginning of the world, God was determined to save people through the death of Christ, and to combine both believing Jews and Gentiles into His church.

Paul the Apostle

Without the Apostle Paul, the apostolic order and Christian religious movement might well have died in its infancy and the world's history since the first century would have been radically different. The Christian faith was grounded on the person of Jesus and his proclamation of the Kingdom of God, and the church as a community and institution was founded on the belief in his resurrection and the hope and expectation of his return. However much it may have flourished under the leadership in Jerusalem of James, the brother of Jesus, Jewish Christianity with its devotion to the Temple, synagogue, and the Law, seems to have effectively disappeared from history before the close of the first century. It was the Gentile or Hellenistic Christianity, firmly established through the missionary efforts especially of Paul, that survived to become the mainstream of historical Christianity, not only of the Catholic Church but of the major heretical movements—Montanism, Marcionism, Nestorianism, and Arianism.[8]

Although his conversion to Christianity was a turning away from some basic commitments to Judaism, even as a Christian and as the chief creator of Christian theology Paul did not abandon his fundamental allegiance to the Jewish religious tradition. His religion as a believer in Christ became a religion of grace rather than law, but he remained committed to the monotheistic foundations of Judaism and to the moral principles of the Hebrew

---

[8] The Coptic Christianity of Egypt, which eventually extended to Nubia and Ethiopia and sent missionaries to Europe, the British Isles, and Arabia, was according to tradition originally established by St. Mark, the reputed author of the Gospel of Mark. See Eusebius, Ecclesiastical History, Bk. II, ch. XVI. See Aziz Atiya, A History of Eastern Christianity (London, 1968), for an extended account of the origins and history of Coptic Christianity.

prophets. His reverence for Moses and the Hebrew patriarchs, Abraham and Jacob, and his devotion to the Hebrew scriptures were typically Jewish. He understood and shared the popular eschatological expectations of his time. Christianity was for him the consummation of Judaism, the continuation of God's chosen lineage until the end of the age. Christ crucified and risen was the fulfillment of the promise.

In Acts of the Apostles the unique status of the Jerusalem church is emphasized. Here Paul is represented as accountable to the leadership in Jerusalem, a base of operations and center for the Christian communities. However, according to Paul's letters, Ephesus, not Jerusalem, seems to have been the headquarters for much of his ministry. On several occasions he went to Jerusalem but primarily to confer with the leadership there. The authority of the Twelve over the entire Christian movement is also asserted in the Acts account, and Paul is represented as submissive to the Jerusalem council. However, on the witness of Paul's own letters, he was not submissive, nor did he consider his authority inferior to that of the Jerusalem council. In Acts the trend is toward the recognition of a formal, authoritative body, the Apostles, whose status and role were enhanced and formalized as an apostolic council. Luke shows Paul accepting the preeminence of the Jerusalem Council led by James, the brother of Jesus, and Peter.

Paul lived during a critical time for the infant church; his letters speak of much internal conflict and strife. He felt strongly about rival factions developing among Corinthian Christians and about the Judaizers, presumably Jewish Christians from Jerusalem who were undermining his efforts in Galatia. According to his letters, decisions important to the church were pending. The precarious condition of the Christian congregations, Paul's relation to them, and the threat posed to the unity of the early church by its internal disputes—all of which appear so clearly in Paul's letters—seem to have been intentionally glossed over in Acts. This book was apparently written in retrospect, some time after Paul had faced the crucial issues of his day.

Three elements of Hellenistic thought and practice are of particular importance for any analysis of the religious concepts of Paul: Graeco-Roman Stoicism, which in this period was a major philosophical movement; the Oriental mystery cults that were increasingly important, especially in the eastern part of the empire; and the Gnosticism which pervaded much Hellenistic religion. To what extent these movements affected Paul's religious attitudes and belief has long been a matter of scholarly dispute. If they influenced him, questions remain about whether he borrowed directly from Stoic literature, for instance, or simply imbibed Stoic ideas from the philosophical atmosphere in which he lived; whether the similarities between his teachings on salvation and some of the popular beliefs of the mystery religions were influenced by one or more of the prevalent mysteries or were simply additional evidence of what was becoming commonplace belief and practice relative to the ultimate destiny of the human soul. The extent to which Paul was influenced in the cosmic and psychological dimensions of his theology is a matter of debate, but that there were important gnostic facets of his thought is obvious.

The conversion experience was for Paul the basis for his authority; it made him a witness to the resurrected Christ and this qualified him as an apostle. Paul does not distinguish between the validity of his own experience and that of the other apostles. Peter and James the brother of Jesus were leaders of the Jerusalem church. But for Paul even their personal intimate relationship with Jesus carried no greater status than his own vision of the risen Christ.

> *"For I delivered to you as of first importance what I also received, that Christ died for our sins in accordance with the scriptures, that he was buried, that he was raised on the third day in accordance with the scriptures, and that he appeared to Cephas [Peter], then to the twelve.... Then he appeared to James, then to all the apostles. Last of all, as to one untimely born, he appeared also to me.... I worked harder than any of them, though it was not I, but the grace of God which is with me". (1 Cor 15:3-5, 7f., 10.)*

Nevertheless, there is a singleness of purpose and meaning which characterizes Paul's writing about salvation. Salvation comes through the risen Christ. With him and in him the converted soul dies to sin and, is justified by God's grace, rises again to the glory of eternal life. This Christocentric conviction of salvation ruled his life as a passionate missionary and became not only the main foundation of traditional Christian theology but the chief moving power of the Christian religion.

The foundation of Paul's thought and feelings is found in Romans 7. Here Paul provides his account of the human predicament, derived from analysis of his own existential dilemma:

"I do not understand my own actions. For I do not do what I want, but I do the very thing I hate. Now if I do what I do not want, I agree that the law is good. So then it is no longer I that do it, but sin which dwells within me. For I know that nothing good dwells within me, that is, in my flesh. I can will what is right, but I cannot do it. For I do not do the good I want, but the evil I do not want is what I do. Now if I do what I do not want, it is no longer I that do it, but sin which dwells within me.

So I find it to be a law that when I want to do right, evil lies close at hand. For I delight in the law of God, in my inmost self, but I see in my members another law at war with the law of my mind and making me captive to the law of sin which dwells in my members". (Rom 7:15-23.)

The Holy Spirit inspired the Apostle Paul to explain the process of becoming a God ordered church. The church is to be a holy temple, an original tabernacle that provides a place where God can meet with man and be worshipped.

The Church's Commission

The church today exists in two forms:

    A. The universal or apostolic church: All believers from the day of Pentecost (Acts 2) to the rapture (1 Thessalonians 4:13-18).

        1. Christ promised to form the Church (Matthew 16:18).

        2. The Holy Spirit "baptizes" – places people into the "body of Christ," which is the universal church (1 Corinthians 12:12-14,27). This function of the Holy Spirit began at the day of Pentecost (Acts 1:5; 2:1-4; 11:15-18).

B. A local church: A group of believers in this age meeting regularly and organized biblically to do God's will. (Examples: Romans 16:1,3-5,14-16).

Jesus preached the Kingdom of God. The Church and the Kingdom are not the same. The Kingdom is eternal and the driving force of Heaven on earth through the Holy Spirit. The original church was never intended to be a religious organization but the agency to bring Heaven to earth.

The purpose of the church is to carry on the work of Christ, being the chief cornerstone in proclaiming the gospel and being a light to the world (John 14:13-14; Acts 1:8; Acts 13:47). The Ecclesia, called out, chosen, and appointed ones, the members of the Body of Christ are mandated to bring the Gospel to all the earth. The gospel was charged to the apostles to spread the good news and to disciple others to do the same. God intended the message of the Kingdom of God be the central thesis and point of the good news. God created mad to glorify Him, and this is to be done by carrying the apostolic teachings God intended according to His order to all nations. Thus the gospel and its life transforming character stand at the heart of the church and is to be reflected in her members. The church is to have a God ordered focus in worship, teaching, and leading others into the apostolic teachings of Christ. This involves freely worshipping the Trinitarian God and praying for each other as well as for those in the world, including our political leaders (1 Tim 2:1-3).

The church is also commissioned to establish and equip new believers in the faith based on the teachings of Christ. This includes teaching concerning the gospel and its ethical concomitants, i.e., obedience to the Lord's commands, love for each other, and responsible and holy living in a fallen world. The church is an organism made of living members of the Body of Christ. The Church is to administer, rule, as God's ambassadors, for we are in the world but not of the world. The church is also to have, as we stated earlier, a consistent ministry to the world in terms of acts of kindness and witnessing to the truth and reality of God and the gospel. Thus a God ordered apostolic church keeps it's focus on the example God, and Jesus, established according the teachings of Paul. Its upward, inward, and outward calls for the order of God as really three aspects of one call to know Christ and to make him known. The primary authority in directing these activities is, of course, is dominion given by Jesus Christ, knowing the apostolic order of God, the Scriptures as interpreted and applied through dependence on the Spirit and the wisdom gained from the knowledge of the command given by Jesus Christ, "Go".[9]

The evidence thus far considered seems to demonstrate beyond all question that the hierarchical organization of the Church was, in its essential elements, the work of the Apostles themselves which is again, God's intended order.. This hierarchy they handed on the charge entrusted to them by Christ of governing the Kingdom of God, and of teaching the revealed doctrine. They are unanimous in holding that the idea of a Church, an organized society, is entirely foreign to the teaching of Christ.

In the course of the nineteenth century many theories were propounded to account for the transformation of the Apostolic order of God into the Christianity of the commencement of the third century. Greater regard is shown for the claims of historical possibility and for the value of early Christian evidences. At the same time it is to be observed that the reconstruction's suggested involve the rejection of the Pastoral Epistles as being documents of the second century. It will be sufficient here to notice one or two points in the views which now find favor with the best known.

It is held that the official organization of God's apostolic order as existed in the Christian communities was regarded as involving special spiritual gifts. Some writers, as has been seen, believe with Holtzmann that in the *episcopi* and *presbyteri*, there is simply the synagogal system of *archontes* and *hyperetai*. Others, with Hatch, derive the origin of the episcopate from the fact that certain civic functionaries in the Syrian cities appear to have borne the title of "episcopi".

---

[9] For further discussion of these three representative forms of church government, see Erickson, *Christian Theology*, 1069-83; Leon Morris, "Church Government," in *Evangelical Dictionary of Theology*, ed. Walter A. Elwell (Grand Rapids: Baker, 1984), 238-41; D. MacLeod, "Church Government," in *New Dictionary of Theology*, ed. Sinclair B. Ferguson, David F. Wright, and J. I. Packer (Downers Grove, IL: InterVarsity, 1988), 143-46.

Professor Harnack, while agreeing with Hatch as to the origin of the office, differs from him in so far as he admits that from the first the superintendence of worship belonged to the functions of the bishop. The offices of prophet and teacher, it is urged, were those in which the primitive Church acknowledged a spiritual significance. These depended entirely on special charismatic gifts of the Holy Ghost.

The government of the Church was thus regarded as a direct Divine, God ordered rule, by Jesus Christ being the chief cornerstone, with the Holy Spirit, acting through His inspired agents. And only gradually, it is supposed, did the local ministry take the place of the prophets and teachers, and inherit from them the authority once attributed to the possessors of spiritual gifts alone (cf. Sabatier, Religions of Authority, p. 24). Even if we prescind altogether from the evidence considered above, this theory appears devoid of intrinsic probability. A direct Divine rule by "charismata" could only result in confusion, if uncontrolled by any directive power possessed of superior authority. Such a directive and regulative authority, to which the exercise of spiritual gifts was itself subject, existed in the Apostolate, as the New Testament amply shows (1 Corinthians 14). In the succeeding age a precisely similar authority is found in the episcopate. Every principle of historical criticism demands that the source of episcopal power should be sought, not in the "charismata", but, where tradition places it, in the Apostolate itself.

- It is to the crisis occasioned by Gnosticism and Montanism in the second century that these writers attribute the rise of the Catholic system. They say that, in order to combat these heresies, the Church found it necessary to federate itself, and that for this end it established a statutory, so-called "apostolic" faith, and further secured the episcopal supremacy by the fiction of "apostolic succession", (Harnac, Hist. of Dogma, II, ii; Sabatier, op. cit., pp. 35-59). This view appears to be irreconcilable with the facts of the case. The evidence of the Ignatian epistles alone shows that, long before the Gnostic crisis arose, the particular local Churches were conscious of an essential principle of solidarity binding all together into a single system.

Moreover, the very fact that these heresies gained no foothold within the Church in any part of the world, but were everywhere recognized as heretical and promptly excluded, suffices to prove that the Apostolic faith was already clearly known and firmly held, and that the Churches were already organized under an active episcopate. Again, to say that the doctrine of Apostolic succession was invented to cope with these heresies is to overlook the fact that it is asserted in plain terms in the Epistle of Clement, c. xlii.

The Church's mission is based on the Scripture passage referred to as the Great Commission and is found in Matthew 28:16-20.

The purpose(s) of the local church are derived by looking at New Testament commands given to the disciples (who were the "foundation stones" of the church; Ephesians 2:20) and other instructions given to individual churches or church leaders.

A. Central Passage – "The Great Commission" (Matthew 28:19,20) Matthew 28:19 & 20 (and the similar "commissions" in Mark 16:15; Luke 24:45-47 and Acts 1:8) are central to the church's purpose. They were spoken by Christ, the Head of the church (Matthew 28:18). They were spoken to the first leaders of the church (Matthew 28:16). And these words were spoken at the crucial time just after Christ arose and before He ascended. Matthew 28:19 & 20 is examined here because it is the most comprehensive of the "commission" passages.

1. The Command – "Go and make disciples"

    a. These two words combine to make a single command that describe what we, the church, are to be doing. ("Go" is a participle and some prefer to translate it "going." But its position in the sentence before the command makes it grammatically linked to "make disciples." Thus it is probably meant as a double command – "Go and make disciples.").

    b. "Go" means that we must take the initiative. Evangelism is required to accomplish the task of disciple-making.

c. "Make disciples" means "make followers, learners." This seems to include the entire process of helping a person understand the gospel of salvation through Christ and then to help them grow as a Christian. The church (every person in it) is responsible for carrying out this command. Every ministry in a church must be part of the process of disciple-making.

2. The Means – "Baptizing, Teaching"

- How are disciples made? It's more than just sharing the gospel. When a person trusts in Christ as Savior, he/she has just begun to be a disciple. These two words explain the means by which Christians grow as disciples.

a. "Baptizing" – Public identification with Christ

- This refers to water baptism, since it is the disciples who are doing it. Water baptism in the New Testament follows salvation and publicly shows our identification with Christ. This is a necessary step in disciple making. In fact one does not find an unbaptized believer in Scripture after the church begins (Acts 2:41, etc.). Baptism will be discussed more under "Ordinances."

b. "Teaching" – Learning the scripture for the purpose of applying it

- The teaching of God's Word is with the goal that people obey it ("teaching them to observe" = do).

2 Timothy 3:15-17 – "know the Holy Scriptures" -----> "reproof, correction, training"

2 Timothy 4:2 – "Preach the Word" -----> "reprove, rebuke, exhort"

James 1:22 – "doers of the Word and not hearers only"

B. A local church purpose statement

- A local church is responsible to carry out, among its people and in areas of influence, the purposes that God has for the universal church. Baptizing is one part of that responsibility (to be discussed). The rest of the church's purpose involves teaching the Word of God to accomplish various goals. The following is a suggested purpose statement of a local church.

STATEMENT: To Glorify God by *Reaching* people with the gospel, *Building* them in their relationship with God and *Involving* them in God's plan (RBI).

To "Glorify God" is the overall purpose. The Bible says "*Whatever you do, do it all for the glory of God.*" (1 Corinthians 10:31 NIV). In other words, any effort of a church must serve not to promote itself but God's greatness.

However, a local church should seek to glorify God in the following ways:

1. Reaching (Acts 11:19-21; Ephesians 4:11)

God has provided the way so that a person can go to heaven and know it. Christ died to pay for our sin. We can go to heaven if we place our trust in Christ's death for us (John 3:16). That truth is central to why a church exists. A church must effectively present the Gospel in various ministries and train others to do so personally. Part of the task includes taking that message around the world through missionaries. But once a person is *reached* with the Gospel, God obviously has more in mind for their life...

2. Building (Acts 11:22-26; Ephesians 4:11-16)

"**Building**" refers to the spiritual process of God bringing the growth and change that we need in our lives. How can a church help to encourage that work of God?

Worship – We exist not for our benefit, but God's glory. So worship must please God by giving God the credit He deserves for His greatness. God cannot "grow" us without an intimate relationship with us. Personal and group worship encourages us to develop that relationship with God.

Instruction – The food we need to grow spiritually is God's Word the Bible (I Peter 2:2). That's why Bible teaching must be central in a local church. A church must provide biblical truth that each person needs and even more importantly to encourage people to study God's Word themselves.

Fellowship – Real spiritual growth requires more than just information. It requires relationships. God has designed that believers need one another to grow. It is through the frustration and diversity of relationships with people that God can best bring us to maturity. So it is essential to have ministries that go beyond a worship service. Personal interaction lets us in on the struggles, joys of other Christians and gives us an opportunity to support each other.

3. Involvement (Acts 11:27-30; Ephesians 4:11,12)

Sometimes people in churches assume that ministry is the job of paid professionals – the pastors and staff. It's not. God has called every believer to be involved in ministry. He has given every person certain "spiritual gifts" – supernatural abilities to serve/help others in some way. Instead of leaders *doing* most of the ministry, their real role is to *equip* people for ministry (Ephesians 4:11,12). Ministry is not an issue of mere duty. It's a matter of gratefully using the gifts/abilities God gives us.

CHAPTER VI.
CHURCH STRUCTURE AND BEYOND

<u>The Ordinances of The Church</u>
    A. Common questions about ordinances/sacraments
        1. What is an ordinance?

            An ordinance is a physical ritual prescribed by Christ to illustrate a spiritual reality (sacrament = sacred sign).
        2. How many ordinances should be practiced?
            Some believe there are up to seven.
            Most Protestants believe there are only two (Lord's Supper and baptism). Why?
            - Only these two are specifically prescribed by Christ and clearly practiced by the early church.
            - Only these two symbolize the saving work of Christ.
        3. What do they have to do with a person's salvation?
            - Practicing these "symbols" in no way saves or even helps a person have eternal salvation (<u>John 3:16</u>; <u>Ephesians 2:8,9</u>).
            - These ordinances are meaningful only to a person who has already personally trusted Christ for salvation.
    B. Water Baptism

1. Definition: The use of water to symbolize outwardly the inner spiritual change that took place when we trusted Christ as Savior.
2. The Model: Baptism was commanded by Christ and practiced by the early church.
   a. Christ commanded the disciples to "Go and make disciples" by means of "baptizing" and "teaching" until "the end of the age" (Matthew 28:19,20).
   b. Starting at the Day of Pentecost (Acts 2:38,41) water baptism after conversion became standard practice (Acts 8:12,36-38; 9:18; 10:47,48; 16:14,15,33; 18:8; 19:4,15).
3. The Meaning: Baptism symbolizes what happened when we were saved.
   a. It symbolizes the Holy Spirit's work of regeneration (making us spiritually new – Titus 3:5). = "I am a Christian."
      - Spirit (real) baptism is done by the Holy Spirit inwardly when we trust Christ as savior (1 Corinthians 12:13; Galatians 3:26,27).
      - Water (ritual) baptism is administered by others outwardly after we're saved (Acts 8:3).
   b. It symbolizes our new life of union with and identification with Christ (Romans 6:3-11). = "I intend to live like a Christian."
4. The Method: Immersion in water anytime after conversion seems most appropriate.
   a. Immersion fits the significance (Romans 6:4) and early examples of baptism (Acts 8:38,39).
   b. New Testament examples of baptism are done immediately after a person is saved (Acts 2:41; 8:12,36-38; 9:18; 10:47,48; 16:14,15,33; 18:8). So when a person is

saved and realizes the significance of baptism, it would seem to be the right time.

  c. Young children who are saved might wisely wait until they understand the significance of baptism. There is no biblical support for baptizing infants with water.

C. The Lord's Supper

 1. Definition: The regular use of the bread and cup to symbolically commemorate with other believers the saving work of Christ on the cross.

 2. The Model: Christ initiated it at the Last Supper.

  a. Christ gave the final two elements of that passover meal a new significance to be practiced after His death (Luke 22:7-20).

  b. This ordinance is a command ("Do this" – 1 Corinthians 11:24,25) to be practiced regularly ("as often as" – 1 Corinthians 11:25,26) throughout this church age ("proclaim the Lord's death until He comes" – 1 Corinthians 11:26).

 3. The Meaning: The Lord's Supper is a memorial to Christ's saving work on the cross.

  a. The bread represents Christ's substitutionary death in our place ("for you" – Luke 22:19; 1 Corinthians 11:24).

  b. The cup represents Christ's fulfilling of the old covenant sacrifice system ("the new covenant in my blood" – Luke 22:20; 1 Corinthians 11:25).

 4. The Method:

  a. The early Church's form

   - The love feast (a shared meal – 1 Corinthians 11:20-22)

   - The elements (a shared loaf and cup – 1 Corinthians 11:23-25).

   - Done weekly as the church gathered ("breaking of bread" – Acts 20:7,11).

  b. The basic function required

The Lord's Supper should be practiced regularly by churches using similar symbols with the identical significance Christ gave them.

The Structure of the Church

The church is not merely an organization. The universal church, as we have seen, is an "organism." That is, the church is first of all a living spiritual unit – the body of Christ. But on a local level, churches must be organized to do God's will. This discussion will survey the various views of church structure and make some biblical observations.

   A. Major views of church structure

      1. The hierarchical view – This view holds that the authority in local churches rests in "bishops" who oversee several local churches. The bishops then have authority over local ministers who they ordain and appoint, who in turn have authority over the congregation.

         a. Roman Catholics, state churches (church of England, etc.), the Episcopal Church hold this view. Many other denominations also rely to some extent on authority from above and outside of the church.

         b. Proponents use passages such as <u>Acts 15:13ff</u>; <u>1 Corinthians 4:17</u>; <u>2 Corinthians 8:23</u> to support the view. Those passages describe how the apostles gave authority to others (Timothy, Titus, etc.). But never was that authority said to be passed on further.

      2. The federal view – This view is also called "elder rule" because that's where the authority lies. Elders receive authority by being elected from the congregation or being appointed by fellow elders.

         a. Presbyterians and Reformed groups hold this view (although they are organized on a denominational level as well). Many independent churches also follow this form to a large degree.

b. The scriptural support for the concept is found in the overall sense of authority invested in elders (1 Timothy 3:1-7; 5:17; Titus 1:5-9; 1 Peter 5:1-5, etc.).

3. The congregational view – This view holds that the congregation holds final authority on all matters. The pastor and other leaders are elected by the congregation to teach and lead but the congregation has authority over them.

    a. To a greater or lesser degree most Protestant churches have some elements of the congregational view. Some churches (Independents, Baptists and others) adhere to it very strictly.

    b. Proponents point to the fact that only Christ is above the congregation as "Head" of the church (Ephesians 5:23). They also point to the priesthood of believers (Hebrews 10:19-22; 1 Peter 2:5-9) and references to matters handled by the congregation (deacons selected – Acts 6:5; discipline – 1 Corinthians 5:1-5, etc.).

B. Determining a biblical view of church structure

  1. Who has authority in local church matters?

    - None of the above views is the only true biblical view. There is a clear biblical evidence for elements of elder rule and congregational rule. This discussion seeks to understand how both the congregation and the elders were meant to function in terms of authority.

    a. The apostles had authority in the 1st century.

      1) They appointed elders (Acts 19:23).

      2) They settled doctrinal disputes (Acts 15).

  3) They established churches (Paul).

4) They revealed God's will concerning financial support of elders (1 Timothy 5:17) church order in meetings (1 Corinthians 14:40) collections (1 Corinthians 16:1,2) etc.

b. Elders had the highest authority after the apostolic age.

1) Paul put elders in charge in churches (Acts 14:23).

2) Paul told Titus to appoint elders (Titus 1:5).

3) The church is told to obey its spiritual leaders (Hebrews 13:17).

4) "Elder" and "overseer" are interchangeable terms (Acts 20:17,28; Titus 1:5,7; 1 Peter 5:1,2), indicating their role in authority.

5) "Ruling" was one role of elders (2 Timothy 5:17).

c. The local church as a unit had authority.

1) They selected deacons (Acts 6:3-5).

2) They sent Paul and Barnabas to help settle a doctrinal dispute (Acts 15:2,3) and then confirmed, with the other elders, how the issue should be settled (15:22).

3) They administered church discipline (1 Corinthians 5:5; 2 Corinthians 2:6,7).

4) They sent out missionaries (Acts 11:22; 2 Corinthians 8:19).

d. Conclusions

1) A biblical view would seem to include elements of elder rule and congregational rule. The apostles had authority over local churches but they never established a system of hierarchical rule.

2) The model for church government must come from scripture not from examples of civil government. (ie. The church is not to be a democracy just because America is.) The goal of church decision-making is not to determine the will of the majority but to determine the will of God.

3) God has designed His spiritual "organism" – the church – to be led by spiritually qualified leaders (see qualifications). They do indeed direct the church's ministry toward God-given goals. Spiritual leaders are initiators.

4) The congregation as a whole was gathered to decide on some very significant issues (see above) so it seems that a local congregation today would also be involved in weighty matters.

5) Each church has to decide how much decision-making is done at the leadership level and what is done at the congregational level. Some issues are of such a nature that it would be unwise to involve the whole congregation. Some issues are of such a nature that it would be unwise not to involve the whole congregation. But godly qualified leadership is key. When spiritual leaders have courage to lead and sensitivity to the needs of the congregation, God is free to produce harmony and effective spiritual ministry.

2. Should churches organize above the local church level?

- This discussion concerns the issue of whether churches should function together as denominations or as autonomous (self-governing) independent churches.

a. Biblical information and example

1) The apostles coordinated group efforts to meet the financial needs of the poverty-stricken Jerusalem church – (1 Corinthians 16:1-4; 2 Corinthians 8:1-9:15). Also, Paul was supported by several churches, although each church made their own decision about giving (Philippians 4:15; 1 Corinthians 9:12; 2 Corinthian 11:9; 12:13).

2) When the church at Antioch experienced a doctrinal conflict about what was required of Gentiles to be saved, the church asked for help from the spiritual leaders at Jerusalem. Their decision solved the problem (Acts 15)

b. Conclusions
> 1) The early church examples of financial cooperation and mediation of a conflict are good models of how like-minded churches can help each other.
>
> 2) These examples do not, however, establish a structure of authority. Churches were designed by God to have the gifts and leadership they needed to function on their own (1 Corinthians 1:7). Denominations can certainly function in a biblical way in accomplishing God's purposes, while many believe that independent, autonomous churches are closest to the biblical model, and best able to do the unique ministry God gives them in a local area.

Church's Mission

The Church's mission is to preach the gospel of the Kingdom of God and His righteousness, and to make disciples throughout the world, teaching them exactly what Jesus taught. The work of the Church continues. It did not cease when the original disciples died. The Church's mission has passed to each generation of God's people. Jesus promised to be with His followers as they accomplished that work until He returns at the end of the age. The church as a company of believers is to be active and aggressive in winning the lost. The church is commanded to teach its disciples to observe all things that Christ commanded.

Paul describes the Church's responsibility as the ministry of reconciliation. God was in Christ reconciling the world to Himself, not imputing their trespasses to them, and has committed to us the word of reconciliation. (II Corinthians 5:18-19). God's ultimate purpose for His church is to gather and to reconcile all mankind to Himself according to His apostolic order. God has commissioned us to preach how reconciliation will occur. We have seen that Jesus Christ told His followers to go into all the world, making disciples of all nations and teaching people about the Kingdom of God and His righteousness. This takes cooperation and organization. To effectively describe the organized functioning of the people of God, the apostles used the analogy of the human body. "Now you are the body of Christ, and each one of you are a part of it. And in the church of God, He has appointed apostles, prophets, third teachers, then workers of miracles.

Later, Jesus Christ inspired the Apostle Paul to explain the process of becoming a God ordered church: The church is to be a holy temple, original tabernacle that provides a place where God can meet with man and be worshipped. So the body of Christ or the Church is to be a dwelling place for God. God is at the center of the body of Christ and the church. Therefore, from the dwelling of God emanates or flows the oracles of God who interpret the order of God for the body of Christ. The church is to be a place of teaching. Christ daily taught the truth about the Kingdom of God in the temple. The early church continued to preach Christ in the temple as well as from house to house. The objective that Jesus has for His Church: make disciples of the nation, preach the Gospel to every creature, preach repentance and remission of sins. The message is preaching and teaching believers how to understand and operate within the Kingdom of God. The oracles of God are our leaders who are misinterpreting the plan of God for His church through the traditions of elders and men.

DR ETHEL REID-SMITH

CHAPTER VII.
THE NEW TESTAMENT CHURCH

The church is a gathering of people, and an assembly. The meeting place is not important, but that they do meet is most important, for here is where Christ carries out His work on earth. The church is the various parts of Christ's body meeting together for mutual help, encouragement, and reinforcement for growing into Christian maturity according to the commands of God's apostolic order. Also, all the parts are working together effecting change, influencing their communities, reaching out to hurting and discouraged people, bringing them healing and salvation through Christ our Healer and Savior.

Jesus Christ desires to establish His New Testament church according to God's intended apostolic order by giving five distinctly different types of calls or offices, five fold ministry, or offices: apostles, prophets, evangelists, pastors and teachers. These offices are not for control or member competition.

1. In the Gospels

Apart from the passage just referred to, the word *ekklēsia* occurs in the Gospels on one other occasion only (Mat_18:17). Here, moreover, it may be questioned whether Our Lord is referring to the Christian church, or to Jewish congregations commonly known as synagogues (see the Revised Version, margin) The latter view is more in keeping with the situation, but the promise immediately given to the disciples of a power to bind and loose (Mat_18:18) and the assurance "Where two or three are gathered together in my name, there am I in the midst of them"

(Mat_18:20) are evidently meant for the people of Christ. If, as is probable, the *ekklesia* of Mat_18:17 is the Christian *ekklesia* of which Christ had already spoken to Peter, the words show that He conceived of the church as a society possessing powers of self-government, in which questions of discipline were to be decided by the collective judgment of the members.

2. In Acts

In Acts the *ekklēsia* has come to be the regular designation for the society of Christian believers, but is employed in two distinct senses. First in a *local* sense, to denote the body of Christians in a particular place or district, as in Jerusalem (Act_5:11; Act_8:1), in Antioch (Act_13:1; Act_15:22), in Caesarea (Act_18:22) - a usage which reappears in the Apocalypse in the letters to the Seven Churches. Then in a wider and what may be called a universal sense, to denote the sum total of existing local churches (Act_9:31 the Revised Version (British and American)), which are Thus regarded as forming one body.

3. In the Pauline Epistles

In the Pauline Epistles both of these usages are frequent. Thus the apostle writes of "the church of the Thessalonians" (1Th_1:1), "the church of God which is at Corinth" (1Co_1:2; 2Co_1:1). Indeed he localizes and particularizes the word yet further by applying it to a single Christian household or to little groups of believers who were accustomed to assemble in private houses for worship and fellowship (Rom_16:5; 1Co_16:19; Col_4:15; Phm_1:2) - an employment of the word which recalls the saying of Jesus in Mat_18:20. The *universal* use, again, may be illustrated by the contrast he draws between Jews and Greeks on the one hand and the church of God on the other (1Co_10:32), and by the declaration that God has set in the church apostles, prophets, and teachers (1Co_12:28).

But Paul in his later epistles has another use of *ekklēsia* peculiar to himself, which may be described as the *ideal* use. The church, now, is the body of which Christ is the head (Eph_1:22 f; Col_1:18, Col_1:24). It is the medium through which God's manifold wisdom and eternal purpose are to be made known not only to all men, but to the principalities and powers in the heavenly places (Eph_3:9-11). It is the bride of whom He is the heavenly Bridegroom, the bride for whom in His love He gave Himself up, that He might cleanse and sanctify her and might present her to Himself a glorious church, a church without blemish, not having spot or wrinkle or any such thing (Eph_5:25). This church clearly is not the actual church as we know it on earth, with its divisions, its blemishes, its shortcomings in faith and love and obedience. It is the holy and catholic church that is to be when the Bridegroom has completed the process of lustration, having fully "cleansed it by the washing of water with the word." It is the ideal which the actual church must keep before it and strive after, the ideal up to which it shall finally be guided by that Divine in-working power which is able to conform the body to the head, to make the bride worthy of the Bridegroom, so that God may receive in the church the glory that is His (Eph_3:21).

IV. The Notes of the Church

1. Faith

Although a systematic doctrine of the church is neither to be found nor to be looked for in the New Testament, certain characteristic notes or features of the Christian society are brought before us from which we can form some conception as to its nature. The fundamental note is *faith*. It was to Peter confessing his faith in Christ that the promise came, "Upon this rock I will build my church" (Mat_16:18). Until Jesus found a man full of faith He could not begin to build His church; and unless Peter had been the prototype of others whose faith was like his own, the walls of the church would never have risen into the air. Primarily the church is a society not of thinkers or workers or even of worshippers, but of believers. Hence, we find that "believers" or "they that believed" is constantly used as a synonym for the members of the Christian society (e.g. Act_2:44; Act_4:32; Act_5:14; 1Ti_4:12). Hence, too, the rite of baptism, which from the first was the condition of entrance into the apostolic church and the seal of membership in it, was recognized as pre-ëminently the sacrament of faith and of confession (Act_2:41; Act_8:12, Act_8:36; Rom_6:4; 1Co_12:13). This church-founding and church-building faith, of which baptism was the seal, was much more than an act of intellectual assent. It was a personal laying hold of the personal Savior, the bond of a vital union between Christ and the believer which resulted in nothing less than a new creation (Rom_6:4; Rom_8:1, Rom_8:2; 2Co_5:17).

2. Fellowship

If faith in Christ is the fundamental note of the Christian society, the next is *fellowship* among the members. This follows from the very nature of faith as just described; for if each believer is vitally joined to Christ, all believers must stand in a living relation to one another. In Paul's favorite figure, Christians are members one of another because they are members in particular of the body of Christ (Rom_12:5; 1Co_12:27). That the Christian society was recognized from the first as a fellowship appears from the name "the brethren," which is so commonly applied to those who belong to it. In Acts the name is of very frequent occurrence (Act_9:30, etc.), and it is employed by Paul in the epistles of every period of his career (1Th_4:10, etc.). Similar testimony lies in the fact that "the *koinōnia*" (English Versions "fellowship") takes its place in the earliest meetings of the church side by side with the apostles' teaching and the breaking of bread and prayers (Act_2:42). The *koinōnia* at first carried with it a community of goods (Act_2:44; Act_4:32), but afterward found expression in the fellowship of ministration (2Co_8:4) and in such acts of Christian charity as are inspired by Christian faith (Heb_13:16). In the Lord's Supper, the other sacrament of the primitive church, the fellowship of Christians received its most striking and most sacred expression. For if baptism was especially the sacrament of faith, the Supper was distinctively the sacrament of love and fellowship - a communion or common participation in Christ's death and its fruits which carried with it a communion of hearts and spirits between the participants themselves.

3. Unity

Although local congregations sprang up wherever the gospel was preached, and each of these enjoyed an independent life of its own, the *unity* of the church was clearly recognized from the first. The intercourse between Jerusalem and Antioch (Act_11:22; Act_15:2), the conference held in the former city (Act_15:6), the right hand of fellowship given by the elder apostles to Paul and Barnabas (Gal_2:9), the untiring efforts made by Paul himself to forge strong links of love and mutual service between Gentile and Jewish Christians (2 Cor 8) - all these things serve to show how fully it was realized that though there were many churches, there was but one church. This truth comes to its complete expression in the epistles of Paul's imprisonment, with their vision of the church as a body of which Christ is the head, a body animated by one spirit, and having one Lord, one faith, one baptism, one God and Father of all (Eph_4:4; Col_1:18; Col_3:11). And this unity, it is to be noticed, is conceived of as a visible unity. Jesus Himself evidently conceived it so when He prayed for His disciples that they all might be one, so that the world might believe (Joh_17:21). And the unity of which Paul writes and for which he strove is a unity that finds visible expression. Not, it is true, in any uniformity of outward polity, but through the manifestation of a common faith in acts of mutual love (Eph_4:3, Eph_4:13; 2Co_9:1-15).

4. Consecration

Another dominant note of the New Testament church lay in the *consecration* of its members. "Saints" is one of the most frequently recurring designations for them that we find. As Thus employed, the word has in the first place an objective meaning; the sainthood of the Christian society consisted in its separation from the world by God's electing grace; in this respect it has succeeded to the prerogatives of Israel under the old covenant. The members of the church, as Peter said, are "an elect race, a royal priesthood, a holy nation, a people for God's own possession" (1Pe_2:9). But side by side with this sense of an outward and priestly consecration, the flame "saints" carried within it the thought of an ethical holiness - a holiness consisting, not merely in a status determined by relation to Christ, but in an actual and practical saintliness, a consecration to God that finds expression in character and conduct. No doubt the members of the church are called saints even when the living evidences of sainthood are sadly lacking. Writing to the Corinthian church in which he found so much to blame, Paul addresses its members by this title (1Co_1:2; compare 1Co_6:11). But he does so for other than formal reasons - not only because consecration to God is their outward calling and status as believers; but also because he is assured that a work of real sanctification is going on, and must continue to go on, in their bodies and their spirits which are His. For those who are in Christ are a new creation (2Co_5:17), and those to whom has come the separating and consecrating call (2Co_6:17) must cleanse themselves from all filthiness of the flesh and spirit, perfecting holiness in the fear of God (2Co_7:1). Paul looks upon the members of the church, just as he looks upon the church itself, with a prophetic eye; he sees them not as they are, but as they are to be. And in his view it is "by the washing of water with the word," in other words by the progressive sanctification of its members, that the church itself is to be sanctified and cleansed, until Christ can present it to Himself a glorious church, not having spot or wrinkle or any such thing (Eph_5:26, Eph_5:27).

5. Power

Yet another note of the church was spiritual *power*. When the name *ekklēsia* was given by Jesus to the society He came to found, His promise to Peter included the bestowal of the gift of power (Mat_16:18, Mat_16:19). The apostle was to receive the "power of the keys," i.e. he was to exercise the privilege of opening the doors of the kingdom of heaven to the Jew (Act_2:41) and to the Gentile (Act_10:34-38; Act_15:7). He was further to have the power of binding and loosing, i.e. of forbidding and permitting; in other words he was to possess the functions of a legislator within the spiritual sphere of the church. The legislative powers then bestowed upon Peter personally as the reward of his believing confession were afterward conferred upon the disciples generally (Mat_18:18; compare Mat_18:1 and also Mat_18:19, Mat_18:20), and at the conference in Jerusalem were exercised by the church as a whole (Act_15:4, Act_15:22). The power to open the gates of the kingdom of heaven was expanded into the great missionary commission, "Go ye therefore, and make disciples of all the nations" (Mat_28:19) - a commission that was understood by the apostolic church to be addressed not to the eleven apostles only, but to all Christ's followers without distinction (Act_8:4, etc.). To the Christian society there Thus belonged the double power of legislating for its own members and of opening the kingdom of heaven to all believers. But these double functions of teaching and government were clearly recognized as delegated gifts. The church taught the nations because Christ had bid her go and do it. She laid down laws for her own members because He had conferred upon her authority to bind and to loose. But in every exercise of her authority she relied upon Him from whom she derived it. She believed that Christ was with her always, even unto the end of the world (Mat_28:20), and that the power with which she was endued was power from on high (Luk_24:49).

V. Organization of the Church

It seems evident from the New Testament that Jesus gave His disciples no formal prescriptions for the organization of the church. In the first days after Pentecost they had no thought of separating themselves from the religious life of Israel, and would not realize the need of any distinct organization of their own. The temple-worship was still adhered to (Act_2:46; Act_3:1), though it was supplemented by apostolic teaching, by prayer and fellowship, and by the breaking of bread (Act_2:42, Act_2:46). Organization was a thing of gradual growth suggested by emerging needs, and the differentiation of function among those who were drawn into the service of the church was due to the difference in the gifts bestowed by God upon the church members (1Co_12:28). At first the Twelve themselves, as the immediate companions of Jesus throughout His ministry and the prime witnesses of the Christian facts and especially of the resurrection (compare Act_1:21, Act_1:22), were the natural leaders and teachers of the community. Apart from this, the earliest evidence of anything like organization is found in the distinction drawn by the Twelve themselves between the ministry of the word and the ministry of tables (Act_6:2, Act_6:4) - a distinction which was fully recognized by Paul (Rom_12:6, Rom_12:8; 1Co_1:17; 1Co_9:14; 1Co_12:28), though he enlarged the latter type of ministry so as to include much more than the care of the poor. The two kinds of ministry, as they meet us at the first, may broadly be distinguished as the general and prophetic on the one hand, the local and practical on the other.

1. The General and Prophetic Ministry

From Act_6:1 we see that the Twelve recognized that they were Divinely called as apostles to proclaim the gospel; and Paul repeatedly makes the same claim for himself (1Co_1:17; 1Co_9:16; 2Co_3:6; 2Co_4:1; Col_1:23). But apostleship was by no means confined to the Twelve (Act_14:14; Rom_16:7; compare *Didache* 11 4ff); and an itinerant ministry of the word was exercised in differing ways by prophets, evangelists, and teachers, as well as by apostles (1Co_12:28, 1Co_12:29; Eph_4:11). The fact that Paul himself is variously described as an apostle, a prophet, a teacher (Act_13:1; Act_14:14; 1Ti_2:7; 2Ti_1:11) appears to show that the prophetic ministry was not a ministry of stated office, but one of special gifts and functions. The apostle carried the good tidings of salvation to the ignorant and unbelieving (Gal_2:7, Gal_2:8), the prophet (in the more specific sense of the word) was a messenger to the church (1Co_14:4, 1Co_14:22); and while the teacher explained and applied truth that was already possessed (Heb_5:12), the prophet was recognized by those who had spiritual discernment (1Co_2:15; 1Co_14:29; 1Jo_4:1) as the Divinely employed medium of fresh revelations (1Co_14:25, 1Co_14:30, 1Co_14:31; Eph_3:5; compare *Didache* 4 1).

2. The Local and Practical Ministry

The earliest examples of this are the Seven of Jerusalem who were entrusted with the care of the "daily ministration" (Act_6:1). With the growth of the church, however, other needs arose, and the local ministry is seen developing in two distinct directions. First there is the presbyter or elder, otherwise known as the bishop or overseer, whose duties, while still local, are chiefly of a spiritual kind (Act_20:17, Act_20:28, Act_20:35; 1Ti_3:2, 1Ti_3:5; Jam_5:14; 1Pe_5:2). Next there are the deacon and the deaconess (Phi_1:1; 1Ti_3:8-13), whose work appears to have lain largely in house to house visitation and a practical ministry to the poor and needy (1Ti_5:8-11). The necessities of government, of discipline, and of regular and stated instruction had Thus brought it to pass that within New Testament times some of the functions of the general ministry of apostles and prophets were discharged by a local ministry. The general ministry, however, was still recognized to be the higher of the two. Paul addresses the presbyter-bishops of Ephesus in a tone of lofty spiritual authority (Act 20:17:ff). And according to the *Didache*, a true prophet when he visits a church is to take precedence over the resident bishops and deacons (*Didache* 10 7; 13 3).

DR ETHEL REID-SMITH

CHAPTER VIII.
THE FIVE-FOLD MINISTRY

Literature

Hort, *The Christian Ecclesia*; Lindsay, *The Church and the Ministry in the Early Cents.*, lects I-V; Hatch, *Bampton Lectures*; Gwatkin, *Early Church History to ad 313*; Köstlin, article "Kirche" in See Hauck-Herzog, *Realencyklopadie fur protestantische Theologie und Kirche*; Armitage Robinson, article "Church" in *Encyclopedia Biblica*; Fairbairn, *Christ in Modern Theology*, 513-34; Dargan, *Ecclesiology*; Denney, *Studies in Theology*, Ch viii.

Five Fold Ministry

Apostles are leaders and visionaries which bring direction to the church. They have the courage and ability to keep the Church moving forward, growing, and building in new directions. Apostles are also fathers, the are able to nurture and disciple the other ministry giftings. They have maturity and experience beyond their fellows and can give guidance as well as leadership. They wear the Helmet of Salvation, which means they walk within salvation. They know the mysteries of Christ's salvation. Such knowledge is only acquired through time and experience, trials and testing. An apostle is proven by his example of holiness and demeanor in Christ Jesus. The Helmet of Salvation is not a royal crown. It is the hat of a warrior general who is accustomed to putting his life on the line, for the sake of the Kingdom of God. Many who are in this office will never be recognized as apostles. The reason is this, when a man is truly led by God to establish a work of any kind, it may bristle against the establishment.

The Apostle Paul is a good example of a man on a mission from God, Listening to God is not easy, it can cause you to be treated like an outsider and at times even a rebel! I believe men that are in the office of Apostle are always misunderstood and treated like oddballs. Based upon scriptural precedence apostles are usually the recipients of dreams and visions, Apostles receive an abundance of revelation from God, Why? They establish ministries and churches.

It is quite possible to be an Apostle and never pastor a church is a nefarious statement. Contrary to popular belief Paul was never a pastor. Paul was a Teacher/Apostle. Now another shocker is that Peter was not a Pastor either, the Pastor of the church in Jerusalem was James (The Lord's Brother); Peter was an Evangelist/Apostle. Apostles usually carry dual roles! Here is another curve for you Barnabas was an Apostle too, but he was a Deacon/Apostle his ministry was one of service and support yet he was counted as an Apostle.

I do believe that there are Apostles today, men and women that are sent to establish works according to God's divine mandate. Now too many are starting storefront churches and calling themselves Apostle. Real Apostles don't run around calling themselves Apostle. They know it, and they walk in it!

Only sent ones can fulfill the mandate of restoring apostolic order to Gods church. Only sent ones will be able to overcome the impossible odds that stand in the way of being able to say, "I've done the will of God." The Church cannot succeed without operating strongly in this dimension. After the early apostles died, this mandate remained. It has yet to be totally fulfilled and will remain in force until the day it is fulfilled.

If the commission is apostolic, that means only sent ones can fulfill it. Every church and every believer must have this dimension to be a part of fulfilling the Great Commission. This does not make everyone an apostle, but everyone can be *apostolic*.

Those believers called to the five fold ministry will have a greater dimension of the Apostolic anointing in the gift to which they are called.

A characteristic of the apostolic spirit is an *awareness* of being sent. There is a sense of purpose and destiny that results from the apostolic spirit – a focus upon fulfilling a divine commission.

So Jesus said to them again, "Peace to you! As the Father has sent Me, I also send you." And when He had said this, He breathed on them, and said to them, "Receive the Holy Spirit" (John 10:21,22).

The attributes of a sent one should be found in every believer.

Prophets/Prophetess has a strong sense of right and wrong, but even more than that, they have a strong sense of the Spirit's leading. Their spiritual antennae start quivering when things are going off balance or in wrong directions. Their voice is important for keeping the Church on track in what the Lord wants to do. Prophets also understand justice and are defenders of what is fair and right. Prophets carry the Breastplate of Righteousness, which illustrates the passion and conviction that burns deep within their heart and soul and spirit. Righteousness is actually an ethereal word, a supernatural word. True righteousness flows only from the throne of God. Therefore, the insight of the prophet is a very mysterious, deep conviction that is not easily described even by those who walk in this gifting.

The purpose of a prophet is for guidance and revelation, so that the church can learn what it means to be the Holy People of God and following apostolic order. The Prophet/Prophetess must maintain a level of personal holiness that is exemplary. The primary purpose of the prophet is to warn the church of apostasy and help saints press into the holiness and purpose of God. (Elijah and Ezekiel) Unlike the Office of Apostle which is male ordered, Women can function in this office as well as men. (Deborah, Huldah, and Phillip's Daughters)

The Prophet must have an extraordinary prayer life. If you study the life of a Biblical prophet they were often solitary people. (Elijah and Jeremiah) They didn't have a lot of friends, this is on purpose! God needs those in the prophetic office to be focused on HIM! The Prophet and the Teacher are similar in this regard, Prophets focus on the inspired word (Rhema) and the Teacher more on the written (Logos). But if you look at Acts 17:11 the

Bereans understood the importance of both, but they confirmed the Rhema by studying the Logos! Usually God places Prophets and Teachers as friends and companions for this reason.

Evangelists are the warriors, the foot soldiers who take the gospel to urban and remote areas of the world. They advance the gospel and in so doing they battle directly with the hindrances of the gospel as well. There are many more warriors in an army than there are generals and so there must be many, many more evangelists in the church.

Evangelists wear the Shoes of Peace because they bring news of Peace to a world that suffers in strife and turmoil. Every one of the other 5-Fold Ministers must do the work of an Evangelist, because soul-winning is every minister's duty! Too many of our churches have lost sight of the office of Evangelist and have distorted their purpose by calling "Revivalist" Evangelist, there is difference by a mile. An Evangelist is a soulwinner first and foremost. They go into the streets, prisons, hospitals, and mission fields. Many of the people we call evangelist are preaching to people already saved. A revivalist preaches to people already saved to inspire and fire them up. This is more of the ministry of the Prophet. An Evangelists bottom line is reaching the lost and preaching the Gospel of Jesus Christ. The motto of an Evangelist could be a quote from Paul, "Woe unto me if I preach not the Gospel!"

Pastors nurture the flock and comfort them. They build up the sheep in their most holy faith. They tend to the wounded and the sick and have skills for healing. The pastor leads the healthy sheep into good pastures so they will eat well and be strong. And, the pastor looks for the sheep who have wandered away so that none will be lost. Pastors carry the Shield of Faith. Often a warrior was protected by an armor bearer who held his shield for him. In the same way, pastors will shield those who need it until they are strong again. They hover over their flock to build them and strengthen them in the faith. The pastor is not distant from the sheep. The pastor is next to them and among them, holding the Shield in order to deflect the flaming arrows, the weapons, the wild beasts that would destroy. The pastor works one on one so that his sheep will prosper. A flock that prospers is a direct credit to the shepherd who oversees them. A Pastor has to love the sheep, too often people choose Pastors because they can preach well, but eloquence is not the earmark of a great Pastor, it is LOVE.

Pastors have to care for those that are hurting and broken, and at the same time be open to have the other 4 ministry offices share in the ministry. Too often it has been supposed that the office of Pastor is the most important office, but all of the five offices are equally important. A Pastor needs an Evangelist to bring souls into a place where they can be nurtured and fed the sincere milk of the Word of God.

Teachers build the foundations of the church. They minister in the Word of God and remind us of the priorities and foundations that will keep us stable in our lives. They teach the church how to be wise in the ways of God. Both teachers and prophets have a special gift for worship because the prophet can worship in spirit and the teacher can worship in truth and those two characteristics are necessary for true worship. Teachers carry the Belt of Truth, which means they have intimate knowledge of Him who is Truth. A true teacher knows how to give Rhema, which is more than mere words of knowledge. The Rhema word is that which gives Life. Therefore, a teacher knows the One who is the way, the word, the truth, and the life. It is only from this vital relationship that the inspired ministry of the teacher can flow.

Teachers are guardians of Biblical Doctrine (Logos), the Bereans (Acts 17:11) exemplify the character of a Teacher. Teachers search the scriptures. They study the Word more than the average person, there are times when they stay up all night reading entire books of the Bible to determine if something they heard preached in church was accurate. In many cases Teachers are somewhat cold, they care more for truth than unity or peoples feelings. If you remember Paul in Galatians, He read Peter and the Hebrew saints the riot act for the way they allowed the Judaizers to distort the Gospel of Grace.

When a teacher hears a sermon that is off scripturally, it usually drives them crazy. Teachers are like the Scribes of the Old Testament they determined whether every jot and tittle of the Word was correct. Pricilla and Aquilla were teachers and they caught Apollos preaching doctrine that wasn't correct, they pulled him aside and corrected him in love. If a church doesn't have the office of a teacher within its ranks it is in danger of falling into error. (I Tim. 4:1-4) Without a proper foundation, buildings don't stand, civilizations don't last, and Christians don't witness well. That foundation is the foundation of basic Christian doctrine.

The members of Christ's church, His body on earth, are people who believe that Jesus is the Christ the Son of God, obeys the commands of God, and have turned their lives over to Him. They embrace the five fold ministry and apostolic order of God. They have changed lives, for the Holy Spirit is living within them. He is changing their lives from one of sin to one of holiness. They have put off the old body of sin and are producing the fruit of the Spirit, such as love, joy, peace, long suffering, gentleness, goodness, faith, meekness, and temperance.

We would naturally expect every church which claimed to be New Testament to claim that the New Testament was its final charter, the ultimate authority in matters of faith and practice. Strangely, however, when it comes to the matter of the government and ministry of the church, the New Testament is often set aside for what might be called 'practical reasons.' A number of instances men have gone into so-called New Testament churches and practice what directly contradict the Scriptures, but where the people tenaciously hang on to their traditions because 'that's the way we have always done it.'

While some churches are totally adverse to change of any kind, others feel guilty if they are not constantly changing and trying new ideas. Every Sunday Christians go to church wondering what kind of novelty they will find this week because of different traditions.

The Church of the "Baptists, Catholics, Protestants, Lutherans, Evangelical, Jehovah's Witnesses, Seventh day Adventists, Mormons, Orthodox, Quakers, Methodist, Pentecostal, Presbyterian, Calvinism, Arminianism, etc." But, as Paul asks above, "Is Christ divided?" If not, then how can these divided Churches be of Christ?

They may endeavor to be a New Testament church[10] in the fullest sense of the term. But, the New Testament is fully authoritative in not only one's personal life, but also for the corporate life and ministry of the church. This is also the desire of the believers to return to God's intended apostolic order and staying scripturally based.

There have been many failures in the local churches which justify a great deal of criticism. Much of the evangelism which has occurred in recent years is not directly attributable to the order of God. Even worse, a significant portion of the follow-up and fellowship which these new Christians have received has been a result of organizations other than the local church. But these failures do not justify an abandonment of the local church; they necessitate a fresh look at the Scriptures in order to instruct us as to how the church must change in order to conform to the Scriptures, and order that God intended, to once again carry out its task in the world.

By and large, the Lord had not given instructions regarding the church while upon the earth. He spoke about the Millennial Kingdom which He offered and which Israel rejected due to their rejection of Him as its Messiah. Even the last words of our Lord in Acts chapter one are directed more to the kingdom than to the church (cf. Acts 1:3, 6). As our Lord Jesus said, there were many things which His disciples needed to know, but they were not yet able to bear them (John 16:12). These matters would be taught them by the Holy Spirit: "But the Helper, the Holy Spirit, whom the Father will send in My name, He will teach you all things, and bring to your remembrance all that I said to you" (John 14:25-26).

God's apostolic order revealed

Since the doctrines of the church had not been given in the Old Testament or even by our Lord, this doctrine could legitimately be called a mystery, and the Holy Spirit must make these things known only by special revelation. It was the Apostle Paul who was granted the privilege of making these things, God's intended apostolic order known:

---

[10] Henry Clarence Thiessen, *Introduction to the New Testament* (Eerdmans, Grand Rapids, 1943), 253.

In Ephesians 3:1-5, Paul states, "For this reason I, Paul, the prisoner of Christ Jesus for the sake of you Gentiles; if indeed you have heard of the stewardship of God's grace which was given to me for you; that by revelation there was made known to me the mystery, as I wrote before in brief. And by referring to this, when you read you can understand my insight into the mystery of Christ, which in other generations was not made known to the sons of men, as it has now been revealed to His holy apostles and prophets in the Spirit."

It was through the 'holy apostles and prophets' that the Holy Spirit revealed this doctrine of apostolic order for the church, but in the New Testament it is in the epistles of Paul that we come to see the apostolic order of God most clearly defined. Paul wrote the epistles to give specific instruction pertaining to the apostolic order of God to the churches. Many of his epistles are addressed to the churches themselves: "Paul, called as an apostle of Jesus Christ by the will of God, and Sosthenes our brother, to the church of God which is at Corinth" (1 Cor. 1:1-2a, cf. also 2 Cor. 1:1). "Paul and Silvanus and Timothy to the church of the Thessalonians.(1 Thess. 1:1a, cf. also 2 Thess. 1:1; Phil. 1:1).

In addition the so-called 'Pastoral Epistles' were written with the explicit purpose of informing Timothy and Titus how the church was to operate in God's apostolic order during the absence of direct and personal apostolic oversight: "I am writing these things to you, hoping to come to you before long; but in case I am delayed, I write so that you may know how one ought to conduct himself in the household of God, which is the church of the living God, the pillar and support of the truth" (1 Tim. 3:14-15).

Some may say in the New Testament the apostles did it this way, but we don't have apostles any more, so we are not completely sure how it ought to be done. This was precisely the problem faced by Timothy and Titus. Timothy was there at the church at Ephesus, especially with all those who were teaching false doctrine (cf. 1 Tim. 1:3), Well, Paul wasn't there, and I suspect that either Timothy wrote Paul a somewhat frantic letter, or Paul, knowing Timothy as he did, anticipated his anxiety and wrote him this first epistle, followed up some time later by another.

Timothy didn't have an apostle present to tell him what to do, any more than we do today. But what Timothy did have was God's apostolic instruction, the instruction given by inspiration of the Holy Spirit of First and Second Timothy. That is precisely the instruction which we have today. We have no less help and direction than Timothy, indeed we have more, for we have in our possession the entire New Testament.

There is yet one further portion of Paul's writing which I would like to remind you of in connection with this point, and that is in the second epistle to Timothy:

2 Timothy 3:14-17, "You, however, continue in the things you have learned and become convinced of, knowing from whom you have learned them; and that from childhood you have known the sacred writings which are able to give you the wisdom that leads to salvation through faith which is in Christ Jesus. All Scripture is inspired by God and profitable for teaching, for reproof, for correction, for training in righteousness; that the man of God may be adequate, equipped for every good work."

The primary focus of this passage is directed to Timothy as an individual. But there is a secondary emphasis for the church corporately, that the Scriptures are all-sufficient for the church as well as for the individual Christian. In the Scriptures we can find definitive instruction for every essential area of church practice, according to God's apostolic order for example:

- Church conduct and discipline (e.g. 1 Cor. 11; Matt. 5, 18).
- Worship and instruction (1 Cor. 11-14; 1 Tim. 2)
- Church leadership (1 Timothy 3; Titus 1; 1 Peter 5)

Even the silence of the Scriptures is instructive. We not only learn from what the Scriptures tell us, but from what they do not speak to. God deliberately does not tell us how to do everything. This keeps us humble and dependent upon Him to reveal the best possible way of carrying out His will and His word. The Christian life is one of freedom within certain perimeters. What God has not told us He did not want us to know, and we should learn from silence as well as from specific instruction of His order revealed by the Holy Spirit.

Paul's epistles to Timothy and Titus (1 and 2 Timothy and Titus) have generally been called the "Pastoral Epistles."[11] They were originally regarded as mere personal letters and were classified with Philemon, but because of their strong bearing on the life of the church, they gained the name the "Pastoral Epistles." Though addressed to individuals, these books are not limited to personal and private communications, but are somewhat official in character. Paul addressed them to Timothy and Titus to guide them in matters concerning the pastoral care of the church, which is the household of God (cf. 1 Tim. 3:14-15; 4:6-15 with 2 Tim. 2:2).

The term, "pastoral," is an 18th century designation that has stuck down through the years,[2] and though not entirely accurate, it is a somewhat appropriate description of these three letters. Further, due to the large portion of these epistles that deal with church order and discipline, the term "pastoral" is accurate. These epistles deal with church *polity*, *policies*, and *practice*, all of which are concerns vital to the health of the church. However, the term pastoral is inaccurate in the sense that Timothy and Titus were not pastors in the present-day sense of the term. So what were they?

First, these men were official representatives of the apostle Paul whom he dispatched to various churches at Ephesus and Crete. Once there, they functioned in an official apostolic capacity to deal with special situations and meet special needs. During the interim from the time of the apostles to the transition to elders and deacons, these men were sent by Paul as his apostolic representatives to repel and deal with certain conditions and people who were threatening to hurt the work and ministries of these churches.

Second, Timothy and Titus undoubtedly possessed the gifts needed for pastoral ministry and while there was an element of pastoral care in what they did, they were not elders or pastors who are given by the Lord to various churches for long-term ministries (1 Pet. 5:1f). Rather, as official delegates of Paul, they were sent to assist churches in establishing their ministries pastorally-speaking (cf. Tit. 1:5f).

---

[11] *Concise New Testament Survey*, The Biblical Studies Foundation, electronic media, www.Bible.org.

All in all, in their content, these books are pastoral in nature and give directions for the care, conduct, order, ministry, and administration of assemblies of believers. This is true whether they deal with personal matters or the corporate ministry of the church. In summary, then, these books were designed by God to aid us in our pastoral responsibilities and in the organic development and guidance needed for the ministry of local churches.

In this regard there is an important observation that might be made. Of Paul's thirteen letters, these were the very last books he wrote. What is so significant about that? Since these books deal with God's apostolic church order, ministry, and organization, why were they not first? If you or I were doing this (especially today) we would probably first work to get the organization in good administrative order and then worry about the doctrine. So here are some suggestions to think about:

Of course, organization and God's order is important. The church is a spiritual body, an organism. Each believer is a member with special functions and tasks to carry out, but the primary need so essential to functioning as God has designed the church is right theology (teaching) and understanding of the Word, along with its personal application for Christ-like living. This provides us with the spiritual and moral foundation and motivation on which we base our methods, strategy, and administration. So, while our methods will often vary, they must never contradict the moral or spiritual principles of the Word of God which are in accord with godliness, and God's intended order (see Tit. 1:1).

The Apostle Paul practiced what he preached and preached what he practiced. Paul sent Timothy to remind the Corinthians of his ways and what Paul did and practiced. He said that his ways were consistent with his teaching, and this teaching was in Christ. This practice and teaching was not just for the Jewish culture, or the Roman culture, or for the Greek culture, it was to establish the churches according to God's will and to be practiced everywhere, in every church. To keep God's order in the church it must be repeated and reiterated so it is established as the way the church should operate.

We cannot separate God's apostolic practice from God's apostolic principle. Over and over again the apostle made it clear that his teachings and practices did not vary from church to church

(1 Cor. 4:17; 7:17; 14:33; 16:1). Note carefully: I have not said that there is no flexibility in the New Testament, for there surely is. I have not said that the Scriptures spell out precisely how everything is to be done. Neither have I said that there is not room for a diversity of methods which Paul himself illustrates and allows for in others. I have simply said that this matter of simplistically separating apostolic practice from apostolic principle is dangerous and often unbiblical. It would therefore be safe to assume that behind every apostolic practice there is an apostolic principle.

Organization, or better, the organic and unified growth of a church must be based on (1) right teaching, about the apostolic order of God, on teaching that is based on rightly handling the Word, i.e., God's objective truth and (2) on the selection and function of those people who are qualified and spiritually right with God. When we try to run an organization based on tradition or background, we end up with an organization that is not biblical, and lacks the spiritual fervor and capacity to function as God intends.

This book, then, deal with matters of apostolic church order or ecclesiology not hitherto addressed, but before God gave the church directions for church order (or apostolic order as specific as those we find in the pastorals) He gave us Romans, 1 and 2 Corinthians, Galatians, Ephesians, Philippians, and Colossians. Is this because organization is unimportant? No! It is because organization and administration are not primary. They are secondary. Further, it is because sound teaching and spirituality are what ultimately produces ministries that are effective according to God's standards and that manifest the spirit and character of Christ in ministry and outreach.

Several purposes are seen in this epistle. Paul wrote:
> 1. To instruct Titus about what he should do to correct the matters that were lacking in order to properly establish the churches in Crete according to the apostolic order of God.
> 2. To give Titus personal authorization to impart, and teach the view of God's order during the opposition of dissenters Titus was facing (see 2:15; 3:1-15).

3. To give instructions concerning this opposition, to warn about false teachers, and give instructions concerning faith and conduct (1:5, 10-11; 2:1-8, 15; 3:1-11).

4. To express his plans to join Titus again in Nicropolis for the winter (3:12). Whether this meeting ever occurred, we do not know. Tradition has it that Titus later returned to Crete and there lived out the rest of his life.

The theme is to show how the grace of God that has appeared to us in the saving life and death of Christ instructs us to deny ungodliness and to live righteously and soberly as a people full of good works that are in keeping with the doctrine of God's intended apostolic order (1:1; 2:10–3:9).

Important issues discussed in the letter include qualifications for elders (1:5-9), instructions to various age groups (2:1-8), relationship to government (3:1-2), the relation of regeneration to human works and to the Spirit (3:5), and the role of grace in promoting good works among God's people in compliance with His apostolic order (Titus 2:11-3:8).

CHAPTER IX.
THE CHURCH; THE BODY OF CHRIST

The close unity between Christ, the Church and His believers is centered in Christ's Spirit dwelling in each believer/member so they retain their individuality as persons. Just as Christ Spirit indwells in each believer so does the Spirit incorporate God's order. Because the Spirit proceeds from the Father and the Son, He leads and guides us according to God's order.(scripture) Even though each believer has a foundational gift,
these gifts are fitly framed into the body to function in unity.
No one is absorbed by the other, as in Gnosticism.[12] We can see this clearer in 1Cor. 12 where Paul speaks about the role of the Holy Spirit in the Church. In order to emphasize the unity and the variety in the body Christ, Paul says that the variety of the gifts comes "from the Spirit". In the same way as the variety of the services stems from the same Lord and the variety of the workings comes from the same God (1Cor. 12;4-5). "To each is given the manifestation of the Spirit for the common good" (v.7), "who apportions to each one individually as he wills" (v. 11).

The oneness of the Spirit does not lead to the confusion of the various gifts but He unites the operation of the gifts. The same

---

[12] The Gnostics were a sect of philosophers that arose in the first ages of Christianity that formed a system of theology, agreeable to the philosophy of Pythagoras and Plato.

principle, says Paul, applies to the Church which as a body has a variety of members baptized into it "by one Spirit" (I Cor.12:12-13), but with different functions. In the Church, believers "are the body of Christ and individually members of it" (I Cor. 12:24-27). If all were a single organ, where would the body be? As it is, there are many parts, not divisions, yet one body" (I Cor. 12:19-20).

"For by one Spirit we were all baptized into one body, for the body is not one member but many." The apostle Paul sets forth the wonderful truth that church is Christ's body on earth. Based on this truth Paul sets the following teachings concerning the church;

1. God specifically commands that no member of His body think of himself as independently important, and thus given to individual interpretation of God's order. (Rom. 12:3).

2. Each member of the body has his own function. (Rom. 12:4)

3. All members of the body belong to one another. All members, both prominent, and obscure are accepted servants of God, and all are to be honored and respected. (Rom. 12:3)

4. Each member has different abilities given by God. God has given different members various abilities, concerns, insights, and interests. Each has a duty to God to pursue his or her own gift to the glory of God. Paul teaches that each member should concentrate on performing his own job well within the structure of God's order, and not worry about what other members are doing (John 21:20-22).

5. Members have a duty to God to care for one another in the body (I Cor. 12:25, 26).

Christ the Foundation

We serve a global and universal Christ. God's intended apostolic order for His church rings true throughout the universe for conformity. Within God's order are specific steps to follow according to Ephesians the 4th chapter. Equipping the saints/believers for ministry is laid out and specified according to the five fold ministry operations. The gifts in Corinthians are developed by preparation, training, and impartation done by leadership. The design of God's apostolic order for his church was authored through and by Jesus Christ being the chief cornerstone and the foundation on which God's church is built.

The forming of denominations was not the intent of Christ or His apostles. Christianity is a divided religion, composed of hundreds of denominations and schisms. Through the centuries, most of Christianity's branches have assimilated many non-biblical traditions, philosophical, cultural and religious practices into their teachings and practices, spawning even more variations. Because of the different interpretations of the scripture, and ungodly agendas by some leaders the order of the church has become chaotic and ineffective.

Denominationalism

Denominationalism is the system and ideology founded on the division of the religious population into numerous ecclesiastical bodies. Each ideology is stressing particular values or traditions and each competing with the other in the same community under substantial conditions of freedom. Thus denominationalism has usually been associated with religious pluralism, voluntaryism, mutual respect and recognition, and neutrality on the part of the state. *Westminster Dictionary of Church History (1971), pages 262-263.*

As you can see, the very definition of denominationalism goes against the very heart of scripture and God's intended apostolic order. If you compare these words with what scripture says about them, it is all negative: Division (1 Corinthians 1:10-17; 3:3). Traditions (Matthew 15:3,6, Mark 7:8,9,13. Colossians 2:8). Competing (2 Corinthians 10:12). Religious pluralism (Galatians 1:8, 9). Respect (James 2:9, Leviticus 19:15, Deuteronomy 10:17, 2 Chronicles 19:7).

The Bible in no way envisages the organization of the church into denominations. It instead assumes the opposite that all Christians, except those being disciplined, will be in full fellowship with all others. Any tendencies to the contrary were roundly denounced (1 Cor.1:10-13). Paul could write a letter to the Christians meeting in various places in Rome or Galatians with every assurance that all would receive its message and still were operating according to God's order. Today, for any city or country, he would have to place the letter as an advertisement in the secular media and hope. *Elwell's Evangelistic Dictionary of Theology, (1984), page 310.* Articles, Creeds, and Confessions of Faith alike fail to give us this full knowledge of God and His intended order for His church, which is so essential to our faith and walk. They are only man's impressions, inferences, and conclusions drawn from Scripture; and have themselves to be judged by Scripture.

Whatever truth there may be in them, or however useful, they can never take the place of the Word of God or His order. Only in the "person" of the Living Word, and in the pages of the written Word, can we get to know God and His intended apostolic order. *E.W. Bullinger, The Knowledge of God, (1920), page 3.* We should not use any non-scriptural words or expressions. These are the things which divide the members of the One Body, instead of uniting them. They introduce the seeds of strife and contention. These have been the causes of controversies and martyrdom's. *E.W.Bullinger, The Knowledge of God, (1920), page 3.*

Religious denominations actually go contrary to scripture, because they divide Christ (1 Corinthians 1:10-17; 3:3). A kingdom divided against itself cannot stand (Matthew 12:25, Mark 3:24-25, Luke 11:17). In scripture, God's people are called the Christ's assembly. Note: the Greek word *ekklesia* is translated as 'church' in most bibles, but it actually refers to a group of people, and not to a physical building. Therefore, the literal translation is either 'assembly' or 'congregation. For example, "the assembly of God" (Acts 20:28, 1 Corinthians 1:2; 10:32; 11:22; 15:9, 2 Corinthians 1:1, Galatians 1:13, 1 Timothy 3:5), or "the assembles of God" (1 Cor.11:16; 1 Thess.2:14; 2 Thess.1:4), or "the assembles of Christ" (Romans 16:16). God considers naming the name of Christ to be iniquity (2 Timothy 2:19).

Some denominations create a man-made name to place on their man-made Churches. Where is their authority for doing this? 1 Corinthians 1:10-13, "Now I beseech you, brethren, by the name of our Lord Jesus Christ, that ye all speak the same thing, and that there be no divisions among you ; but that ye be perfectly joined together in the same mind and in the same judgment. For it hath been declared unto me of you, my brethren, by them which are of the house of Chloe, that there are contentions among you . Now this I say, that every one of you saith, I am of Paul; and I of Apollos; and I of Cephas; and I of Christ. Is Christ divided? was Paul crucified for you? or were ye baptized in the name of Paul?"

The above verse clearly does not support or give authority to the ideology for systems of denominations. The reason for denominations is because those in the assembly, the church, did not speak the same thing, and that caused divisions among them, and they were no longer joined together. Therefore, they formed different Churches due to the contentions among them. Those in the first century divided themselves and said they were of the assembly of "Chloe, Paul, Apollos, Cephas, etc". Denominations today divide themselves and are completely opposite of what God intended for His church.

The church was a mystery to the Old Testament prophets. The mystery was made known, by the Spirit to His apostles and prophets in the beginning of the dispensation of grace. (Eph. 3:3-6). The mystery of the church was revealed to the apostles after Christ rose from the dead; appeared to them on a mountain in Galilee, and commissioned them to, go and make disciples of all the nations (Matt. 28:19, 20). The apostles were gifted in different areas to minister to different genres of people. But, this did not cause them to teach another gospel. They all taught Jesus being the Lord, Savior and the risen King, thus causing believers to be in order with God's plan for His church. Peter was the first to take the gospel to the Gentiles (Acts 10:1-48).

Paul and Barnabas were the first evangelistic missionaries to the Gentiles. The revelation that Paul received was that a Gentile did not have to become a Jew and follow the tradition of the elders to be in the church. In Christ there is neither Jew nor Gentile, "for you are all one in Christ Jesus" (Gal. 3:28). This was the mystery that was hidden from the men of the Old Testament.

These descriptions revealed in scripture by the Holy Spirit will describe the position of the church as it relates to Christ and God's apostolic order for His church. They are:

1. Christ the Bridegroom, the church His bride in the resurrection will have an incorruptible glorified body (I Cor. 15:51-58), and she will be presented to Him as a pure virgin (II Cor. 11:2; Eph. 5:25-27).
2. Christ the Good Shepherd, the church His sheep. The Shepherd leads, protects, and feeds His sheep (Ps. 23:1-6). When sheep are lost, they cannot find their way back to the sheepfold, they must be sought and found by the shepherd (Luke 15:3-7; John 10:11-16).
3. Christ the Head, the church His body. Christ is the "head of the body, the church" (Col. 1:18). A two-headed anything is not normal, there is only one head of the body or church and He is Christ. His body has many members that serve and minister in different graces, or gifts and offices within the body/church. Christ has complete authority over each member of the body/church.
4. Christ the Foundation and Cornerstone, the church His building. This building is made of "living stones" alive with the life of Christ (I Peter2:5). We are built upon Christ, through the teachings of the apostles and prophets (Eph. 2:19-20).
5. Christ our High Priest, the church His temple. The church is called a "holy temple in the Lord, in whom you are also being built together for a dwelling place of God in the Spirit" (Eph. 2:21-22). Each member of the church is His temple and is indwelt by God the Holy Spirit (I Cor. 6:19-20).
6. Christ the Vine, the church His branches. Jesus said, "I am the vine, you are the branches, (ecclesiola), (John 15:5). In this church age, from Pentecost to the Rapture, every branch is to bear fruit. One of the fruits of a believer is more believers.
7. Christ the Last Adam, the church His new creation. The first Adam was given life; the last Adam is the life-

giver (John 1:4). "Therefore, if anyone is in Christ, he is a new creation old things have passed away; behold, all things have become new" (II Cor. 5:17).

I would like to expand on one comparison, Christ the Head, the church His body. The analogy that Paul uses to describe the Church combines both, the divine and the human. As John says "our fellowship with the Father and with his Son Jesus Christ" became possible by the Son's entrance into world: "that which was from the beginning, which we have heard, which we have seen with our eyes, which we have looked upon and touched with our hands… and the life was made manifest, and we saw it… that which we seen and heard we proclaim also to you, so that you may have fellowship with us" (1John 1;1-3. cf. Phil. 2;5-11. Col. 1;15-20. 1Tim. 3;16 etc.,). This fellowship with Christ is an endless reality for humanity, continuing even after his exultation because it is worked out by the Holy Spirit (John 14,8) and is realized within the Church, since it is the Holy Spirit who makes Christ present in the believers: "Lo, I am with you always, to the close of the age" (Matt.28;20. John 17;11). Because the Church came into being by Christ's presence in the world, Christ's Church is inseparably knit together. This is why the Church's task and mission in the world is "to make known the manifold wisdom of God to the principalities and powers in the heavenly places, according to the eternal purpose which he has realized in Christ Jesus our Lord, …and make all men see what is the plan of the mystery hidden for ages in God who created all things" (Eph. 3:9-11). The Church extends to the whole creation which is thus re-created by joining it.

The common denominator in all these similes is the person of Christ who is the head of the church and body and the author of God's church order. This is how John speaks about them: "Christ is the head, we are the body, …He is the foundation stone, we are the building; he is the vineyard, we are the vine; he is the groom, we are the bride; he is the shepherd, we are the sheep; he is the way, we are the walking ones; we are also the temple, he is the resident; he is the first-born, we are the brothers; he is the heir, we are the co-heirs; he is the life, we are the living; he is the resurrection, we are the risen; he is the light, we are the enlightened" (1 Cor. 8:4).

Belonging to the whole, all parts form a unity and their relationship to one another is defined by the whole which is Christ, this is their generating and formative factor. This reality is better expressed by Paul's metaphor about the Church as "Body", "the body of Christ". This figure of speech called the "body" offers the most appropriate and accurate description of the Church's function as Christ intended it to be. This also is a representation of the extension and continuity of the indwelling of the divine Logos, so that Ecclesiology proper is directly related to Theo-logy, to Soterio-logy and to Eschato-logy. In this way the Church is, as Paul puts it, "the fullness of him who fills all in all" (Eph. 1:22-23). Paul denotes the Church as a living organism, i.e. the body of Christ, and there is no trace of a stage at which he regarded the Church as "body" without considering it as "the body of Christ". This is to say that the Church is a "body" only with reference to the person of Christ.

The first instance in which Paul works out this image of the body, with reference to the Church is 1Cor. 12:12-27 where he concludes (v.27) that Christians form a body as members of it only because they are members of Christ by their appropriation of his saving work of themselves. This makes it clear that the description of the Church as "the body of Christ" is occasioned by the allegory; it was the Church first defined as "the body of Christ" and then the concept of the believers as members of the body was formed. In other words, the believers of Christ who are in Christ are members of the body because they received Christ as their Lord and savior and became a part of the body of Christ which is the Church. Obviously then, this idea clearly gives priority to the personification of Christ in the formation of the body.

The image of the body expresses an ontological entity of a variety of members with different functions but of the same spirit (Rom. 12:4-5. 1Cor.12,12-31. Eph. 4:11-16). What connects the members to each other is not their external similarity and uniformity but the oneness of the Spirit of Christ as explained in I Thessalonians 14, the church of God which is in Christ. Their unity in Spirit, however, does not make them identical as persons, but one in Christ, because in receiving the Spirit of Christ each individual person-member imitates Christ by putting on his own new man free from sin (Gal.3:27) and so enlightened by the Holy Spirit he becomes a son of God by adoption and thus is led into perfection and immortality.

This is what Paul stresses in Rom.6:3-11. The "first fruits of the Spirit" (Rom.8:23. 2Cor.1:22. Gal.4:6. Eph.1:13. Tit.3:5), repeats the event of Pentecost within each individual and so the Holy Spirit filled which proceeds from the Father (God's order) and the son, become "pneumatikos" (1Cor.2:13. Gal.6:1. 1Pet.2:5) by being re-created and reborn into a new life, the life "from above", i.e. "of water and the Spirit" (1 John 3:3-6). It is this radical change affected when the believer is baptized and filled with the Spirit of Christ which attaches every individual in the body of Christ, the Church, where every distinction disappears to the extent that "there is neither Jew nor Greek, there is neither slave nor free, there is neither male nor female; for they are all one in Christ Jesus" (Gal.3:28). Salvation becomes an experience only when man joins the body of Christ, is spirit filled and becomes part of the whole.

Therefore, the individual can become a member only if he belongs to the body of Christ, the Church, in which he is united with him and with the other members. In the Church, his body, the reflection of Christ becomes the nucleus and mitochondria of his believers who do not live to themselves but to Christ to whom they eternally belong (Rom. 14:7-8. Gal. 2:20. 2 Cor. 5:15. Phil.1:21, 1 Pet. 2:4-5), because the life of the head is poured out to its body. This makes it clear why writing to the Corinthians Paul does not ask if the Church is divided, but rather if Christ is divided (1Cor. 1:13. 12,12). In the same sense Christ reproved Saul on the road to Damascus not by asking him why he persecuted the Church, but rather why he persecuted him (Acts 9:4). Again I present the hypothesis, is the church today what God intended it to be?

Many New Testament examples show us our need for God inspired leaders and teachers. Philip's experience with the Ethiopian eunuch clearly illustrates how we need experienced and educated teachers to explain and expound the Word of God and what His order is for His church (Acts 8:26-38). As Philip approaches him, the eunuch is reading an Old Testament prophecy that foretold Christ's sufferings. When asked if he understands the passage, the eunuch has the humility to admit he needs help. He replies, "How can I, unless someone guides me?" (verse 31). Philip then explains to him how this prophecy was fulfilled in the suffering and death of Jesus of Nazareth. This results in the eunuch's baptism (verse 38).

In dealing with the many problems in the Corinthian church, Paul had to send Timothy to refresh them in the truth that Paul had preached. Therefore, I urge you, imitate me. For this reason I have sent Timothy to you, who is my beloved and faithful son in the Lord, who will remind you of my ways in Christ, as I teach everywhere in every church (I Corinthians 4:16-17). The church is going through a transition and God is raising up believers who will speak out and expose man's self-imposed order working in churches. Many times God will send a present day Timothy for correction and they become victims of persecution and ostracizing.

In his letters to Timothy, Paul instructs the young evangelist about various principles that he should teach the people. "These things command and teach.... Teach and exhort these things" (I Timothy 4:11; 6:2). Paul charged Timothy to teach the commands of Christ and not his opinions. In addition, the apostle tells him to train others to be teachers. "And the things that you have heard from me among many witnesses, commit these to faithful men who will be able to teach others, also" (II Timothy 2:2). Besides this, an elder must be "able to teach" (I Timothy 3:2). The very purpose of the ministry is to help in perfecting the saints (Ephesians 4:11-12, KJV).

Throughout the New Testament, God continually emphasizes the need to provide spiritual food to the church. Jesus says that His servants will be providing "food in due season" to His people (Matthew 24:45). "Feed My sheep" is one of the last things Jesus tells Peter (John 21:17). Paul writes to Timothy, "Preach the word! Be ready in season and out of season. Convince, rebuke, exhort, with all longsuffering and teaching" (II Timothy 4:2). The order of God's church was to be reinforced over and over by teaching what Jesus commanded. This tradition should continue to be imitated by each believer and teacher.

In teaching the Corinthians the basic doctrines and order of God, Paul refers to his instruction as milk: "I fed you with milk and not with solid food; for until now you were not able to receive it, and even now you are still not able" (I Corinthians 3:2). The author of Hebrews uses a similar analogy when the brethren needed to relearn God's truth: "For though by this time you ought to be teachers, you need someone to teach you again the first principles of the oracles of God; and you have come to need milk and not solid food" (Hebrews 5:12). The implication of this scripture is at this time the believers should be well versed in the application as well as the implementation of the commands of God.

"And He gave some apostles, and some prophets, and some, evangelists, and some pastors and teachers; for the perfecting of the saints, for the work of the ministry, for the edifying of the body of Christ, ..." (Eph. 4:11-12). In the mentioned verses, the listing of apostles, prophets, evangelists, pastors, and teachers is often referred to as being the five-fold ministry. Each have their own specific function within the body of Christ, yet all accomplish the same three-fold purpose as given in the verse following. What the New Testament saints performed and accomplished then, is no different than what modern day saints accomplish in today's ministry. Malachi 3:6 states "For I am the Lord, I change not...." Since the Lord does not change, then neither does His will, His word or His order.

Given that, then the purpose that a five-fold ministry endeavors to do has not and will not change regardless of how diverse or how multifaceted it may be let us stay in God's order. Yet before one determines to venture out into the realm of ministry, it's best that a clear understanding and definition of ministry be known. Ministry defined in its simplest form, is what one does in service unto the Lord and unto ones fellow man. Conversely, in a much narrower sense, it denotes the officially recognized service of persons set apart (usually by formal ordination) by a church. In both cases, the three-fold purpose is still accomplished and is what will be examined here.

CHAPTER X.
GOD'S PLAN FOR HIS CHURCH

1 – The Perfecting of the Saints for God's Apostolic Order

Someone once said, "practice makes perfect." If we are to live godly lives, we must practice godly living. This is our strongest Christian witness that serves as a powerful evangelistic tool in order to win souls to Christ. Our Lord so instructs us to "Be ye therefore perfect, even as your Father in heaven is perfect" (Matt. 5:8). The word 'perfect' as applied here means to develop fully. Hence, the perfecting of the saints is a growth process. Even our Lord recognized this as evident in the gospel of John in the 17th chapter. It is here that Jesus prays for His disciples a most lengthy prayer, and in verse twenty-three prays that "...they may be made perfect in one; ...". It is a prayer that the followers of Christ be united in "perfect" harmony so that the work of a great coliseum. Another may teach Hebrew in a seminary; another may teach a group of inmates in a prison or in a small home Bible study, or informally on the job, during lunch hour discussions.

We should also seek to define the various spiritual gifts in terms of results, rather than merely in terms of methods. The gift of teaching is not only to be defined in terms of the act of teaching (which has many forms), but in terms of the fruit. The gift of teaching is most evident when people are enriched in their understanding of the Word of God. Some of the most gifted people I know don't necessarily do the things I would associate with their gift, but the fruit of their ministry is obvious. Don't think in terms of the forms of ministry as much as in terms of the fruits of ministry.

Among those who possess the same gift, each will have a unique ministry. My gift will be expressed in a certain environment, deployed through my personality and individuality. Even those whose gifts are identical with mine, and whose ministry is similar, will have differing degrees of effectiveness. You cannot determine your gift(s) merely by studying this subject in the Bible. You must find your gift(s) and specific ministry by ministering, by obeying the commands of Scripture to serve one another. You cannot identify your gift(s) by comparing yourself with others because the ministry of every Christian is unique. While some may have the same gift, their ministries and relative successes will differ.

<u>Determine your priorities on the basis of your spiritual gift(s) and particular ministry.</u>

There comes a time in the Christian's life when there are simply too many needs, too many demands, for him or her to meet. This is the conclusion which the apostles arrived at in Acts 6:3 "But carefully select from among you, brothers, seven men who are well-attested, full of the Spirit and of wisdom, whom we may put in charge of this necessary task. But we will devote ourselves to prayer and the ministry of the word" (Acts 6:3-4). Some have said that it is not necessary for you to know your spiritual gift. Just as each one has received a gift, use it to serve one another as good stewards of the varied grace of God (1 Peter 4:10). Peter tells us that every Christian has received a spiritual gift and that we are stewards of this "grace" of God. How can you be a good steward without knowing your spiritual gift? We must know the gift which God has bestowed upon us to be a faithful steward. We discover what that gift is by ministering to one another.

Church leaders, desperate for workers, frequently make their decisions almost exclusively on availability, rather than on ability or gift. As a result, willing and cooperative Christians are quickly swamped with ministries and commitments. It is at times like this that we must establish some priorities by which decisions can be made.

When your ministry gets to the point that there are more

needs and opportunities than there is time to do them, establish priorities on the basis of your spiritual gift(s). If you are gifted as an administrator, don't get overly involved in some other ministry which will be competitive. While it is wrong to excuse yourself from ministry because you don't know your gift, it is just as wrong to allow a ministry to keep you from that for which you are specially gifted and to which you have been divinely called. As we serve, we should continually evaluate, as best we can, that ministry which has been of greatest benefit to others. (The counsel of others is particularly helpful here.) We should strive to improve and develop the abilities God has given us and give priority to what we do best.

The only way such perfection can come to fruition is if the disciples of Christ practice living godly lives. The concept of this is all perchance best illustrated by a new born infant as to a new convert. A baby will first crawl before it will ever walk. In a similar manner a new convert is to be rooted firmly in Gods Holy word before he/she are to take their own steps, but it takes much practice in living a godly lifestyle before both God and man. Yet it is this type of open witness that will draw others into wanting to know more about the Lord, His love for humanity, an perchance the most important single key element, His saving grace. Whether one is called as an apostle, a prophet, teacher, pastor or evangelist, striving to be perfect will always be a growing process, but it is that growth process produced by a godly lifestyle that will serve as a ministry to others in itself. It may be done at home, on the job, where ever one may go, the idea is to exhibit Christ at all times, The moment one determines in their heart to forego the Christian way of life, the soul loses ground with God and the example that Christ gave us to follow in becomes of ill effect thus damaging what could have been a most dynamic and powerful witness for others to desire and to follow into.

2 – For the Work of the Ministry

Ever hear some would say, "If you don't do it, it won't get done"? Others may declare, "If I don't do it, it won't get done." The bottom line here is obvious; in order for a ministry to function, it will require action. James 2:20 states that "...faith without works is dead." The disciples of Christ went from city to city, town to town, country to country proclaiming Christ, declaring 'good news'. In essence, they were doing the work of an evangelist by teaching God's order for His church. Even if all one does is to teach Sunday School, a most noteworthy ministry, it takes work; it requires action. A ministry is only as good as the amount of effort that is expended to keep it alive. An active, vibrant faith will yield much fruit, whereas little to none reaps what has been sown.

The internal mechanics of any ministry, whether it be street evangelism, nursing home, soup kitchen, or Sunday School, relies solely upon its workers. Matt. 9:37 says thusly, "...the harvest truly is plenteous, but the laborers are few." Therefore, where there is no perfecting of the saints, there is no working ministry; where there is no working ministry, there is no Word, and where there is no Word, mankind is plummeted towards a downward spiral into spiritual darkness and despair. "So then faith cometh by hearing, and hearing by the Word of God." (Rom. 10:17) Thus, in order for a ministry to function, it must have faithful committed laborers, regardless of number who follow God's order.

3 – For the Edifying of the Body of Christ

It's one thing to go forth and "teach all nations, baptizing them in the name of the Father, and of the Son, and of the Holy Ghost..." (Matt. 28:19) and to uplift those who are lost with a message of hope. But, what about edification as Christian to fellow Christian? We can spend all our time, energy, and talent into various evangelistic ministries from street evangelism to global tent revivals, but it will be how Christians treat one another that will ultimately reflect on the ministry to which they are called. Should gossiping, slander, or even a clear and blatant disregard for pastoral of church authority abound; none of which is desirable in the eyes of Almighty God, it will very much so permeate the very core of a church and it ministries. And rather than destroy one another with harsh words or bad attitudes, we are commanded to edify one another. It is the trademark and seal of any Christian ministry. Any Christian can go forth and declare unto others to love their enemy and each other, but the concept starts with the body of Christ.

It is the number one ministry that the saints of God are

charged with by the heavenly Father Himself, and is also the sum total of growing in Christ (perfecting of saints), and ministry laborers who play and active role (work of the ministry) and not a passive one. Hence, Christians are to work together thus culminating in "...the unity of the faith, and of the knowledge of the Son of God, unto a perfect man unto the measure of the stature of the fullness o Christ" (Eph. 4:13). When the objective(s) of a ministry are met, then the purpose as outlined in Eph. 4:12 are met whereby Christians can experience the reward of personal growth and development into the fullness of Christ, as will their ministry to which they have been called.

God's Outline

We are placed in the body of Christ by the Spirit of God. God's nature is expressed in the church through the unity the Godhead, God the father, God the son, and God the Holy Spirit. The believer further expresses God's love not in words only, but in deeds and obedience to His Word. The body of Christ or the Church was designed by God to express His life according to His will. God is perfect. He designed a perfect church that should be the order of our lives. The church that God designed cannot fail, but because the leadership of the church has removed themselves from the authority of God, it seems as though the church has failed. The church is God's creation in Christ Jesus, therefore it cannot fail. Jesus said, "and the gates of hell shall not prevail against the church."

"For by one Spirit are we all baptized into one body, whether we be Jews or Gentiles, whether we be bond or free; and have been all made to drink into one Spirit." (I Cor. 12:13). The design of God for His church is to bring every believer to His plan. The working out of God's plan starts with man being in right relationship with God. The preparation for receiving the Spirit is the believer's acceptance of the sacrificial death of Jesus Christ, and repentance. What results from the plan is our purpose, for He has given us ministry and grace to function in love. To function and come into God's design, we must commit ourselves to God and to what He is doing. Committing to God means I'm

committed to His plan and His apostolic order, and what God is doing is working Himself in us, His body, and the church.

God has created the church, the body of Christ for His purpose. That purpose is that all ministry is given by God and worked by God in the Spirit according to His apostolic order. There is no work done in the body of Christ separate from the Spirit of God, from the giving of ministry to the receiving of ministry and the direction that the Lord gives for order in His church. All working in the body is for God's purpose, not to satisfy man's wants.

Paul tells us in I Corinthians 15:27, 29, how God's purpose will work, *"For he hath put all things under his feet. But when he saith, all things are put under him, it is manifest that he is expected, which did put all things under him. And when all things shall be subdued unto him, then shall the Son also himself be subject into him that put all things under him, that God may be all in all."* God has made every believer alive in every way that He might work all things. We are to know God's plan and design by the revelation of His Spirit and move in it in faith. Peter, after preaching went to the temple and healed a man, all he had was the ministry and gift that God had given him. God knows exactly what it takes to reach the heart of men. When we consult God by His Spirit, he will lead and guide us into the path and direction ordered by God for His church. Without the guidance of God's Spirit, the church will be taken by "every wind of doctrine".

There are so many believers asking what is my purpose? When we would seek God's plan and order for our lives by His Spirit, that question would be answered. God has a plan for every believer, and He wants to order our steps according to His plan. If we as believers desire to know purpose we must first seek God's plan for our ministry according to His will. The saints are all given ministry with a measure of faith. And if the leaders would diligently develop believers they would know the direction in which to go.

The church must take charge of it's destiny and plan, redefine, it's visions, goals, past and plan for the future. Cultures, environments and demographics change. The church must move with the Spirit in its effectiveness of reaching society. We the church must affect where we are by influencing and changing the culture to God designed culture. We must allow the Holy Spirit to speak to us from the Father new ideas to bring earthly exploits. The Holy Spirit himself, nudges us when change should occur. We are being transformed daily let us discern to embrace the change the Holy Spirit is initiating. Condition and environments change, we must adapt our methods using Godly principles to effect change when these dynamics occur.

Defending God's Command

Just as God called Adam in the Garden after he sinned, Jesus is calling His Bride the Church back to His intended plan and order. Saying I am the Lord your God, and I will have no other God before Me. God's plan and order for His church, the body of Christ was created before the earth was formed. The Kingdom of God existed long before the church. The members of God's church do not establish their own order. If they did, confusion would result, for each member is at a different level of growth in knowledge and character. God's church is organized, speaking the same thing, and unified through the authority God has placed in His ministers. The doctrines of God's church come from God through Jesus Christ through the revelation of His Word and His inspiration in the men. He directs His church by His Spirit. Let it be emphasized that the church's purpose is not merely to give salvation to church members—the purpose is to teach and train them to become the instruments God will use to save the vast majority. This is why adhering to God's apostolic order is imperative.

What kind of leadership would it show God to have if He spoke in a confused tongue, as it were, having two men in the same area saying different things about the pathway to the Kingdom of God? God intended apostolic order is that recipe that will form the product at the end of the line if it is believed and if it is applied in one's life through the choices that we make. The doctrine of God is the teaching of His will concerning His plan for His church.

We find here another biblical principle. This is going to be in Mark 3:24. Jesus speaking, He said, "And if a kingdom be divided against itself, that kingdom cannot stand." If God sent two voices or three voices or five voices into the same area at the same time, and they were not speaking the same things, that kingdom is going to be divided against itself and it will not endure. It will split and the factions will be fighting with one another. The factions will say, "*my doctrine is right, not yours. I'm the true church and anybody in those other groups is not the true church*." So <u>pride</u> begins to rise. Vanity takes control. So we snub and ignore other believers of the body of Christ self-righteously thinking that we are better than they.

Mark 3:25-26, "And if a house be divided against itself, that house cannot stand. And if Satan rise up against himself, and be divided, he cannot stand, but has an end." Now God does what He does in order to avoid confusion. There may be periods of time, following the death of a strong leader, where it is not apparent through whom He is working. We can see that from the book of Judges. God raises up a Gideon; Gideon dies. The strong leader leaves, the people go their own way. God raises up another one and the people come together. He dies and the people go their own way.

That has been a pattern that we can see from the very beginning, and during the period that people fall away, there is a great deal of dividing. It's partly because there is confusion about whom it is God is working through. That is why it is so important the mantle of succession be passed to the leader that God has ordained who will obey and lead according to His order and His plan..

CHAPTER XI.
COUNTERFEIT MINISTRY

The church as we know it today does not display what God intended His order to be for the Body of Christ. Chaos, confusion, pride and arrogance is the rule of the day for most denominations and churches. In order to be fitly framed together the body has to mend the holes in the body. When we allow our minds to become stuck, stagnant because of a one time experience set in the past, we are hindered from moving on with God and traditions begin to creep in, making the word of God of no effect **(Mark 7:13).**

Emerging Church Characteristics

Emerging Churches seek to reach the lost by focusing on relationships and developing a "story," a "journey of life" that is expressed through the "narrative" of learning. These words and others are often used by emerging teachers in describing their religious experience. Other terms sometimes used are "reimagine," "tribe," "story of Jesus," "deconstruction," etc. There is sometimes an ambiguous, feelings-oriented desire to experience God and also share in the lives of people as they seek to find God in their way. Some Emerging Churches are inclusivistic (those outside of Christianity will be saved), while others are not. Some Emerging Churches are environmentally focused, while others concentrate on local issues. Some downplay doctrine, reinterpret creeds, and de-emphasize tradition, while others hold to them. Obviously, it is difficult to define precisely what is emerging and what is not.

Seeker-sensitive churches are similar to Emerging Churches except that Emerging Churches are sometimes lax doctrinally, where seeker-sensitive churches, which sometimes are lax in presenting the gospel, hold nonetheless to orthodox theology. Seeker-sensitive churches try to meet people's needs through programs, where Emerging Churches do this by investing time in people's lives. Seeker churches tend to focus on people in their thirties and up where Emerging Churches tend to reach people in their teens to thirties. But, some areas of the Emerging Church are so similar to seeker-sensitive churches that it is hard to tell the difference. So how do you distinguish between the two? Generally, a church is emerging if it seeks to reach those lost in the post-modern culture, rejects doctrinal absolutes, and, of course, proclaims itself to be emerging.

Following are some of the common traits I have discovered by reading through Emerging Church material. But please understand that not all Emerging Churches adhere to all the points listed.

2. An awareness of and attempt to reach those in the changing postmodern culture.
3. An attempt to use technology, i.e., video, slide shows, internet.
4. A broader approach to worship using candles, icons, images, sounds, smells, etc.
5. An inclusive approach to various, sometimes contradictory belief systems.
6. An emphasis on experience and feelings over absolutes.
7. Concentration on relationship-building over proclamation of the gospel.
8. Shunning stale traditionalism in worship, church seating, music, etc.
9. A de-emphasis on absolutes and doctrinal creeds
10. A re-evaluation of the place of the Christian church in society.
11. A re-examination of the Bible and its teachings.
12. A re-evaluation of traditionally-held doctrines.
13. A re-evaluation of the place of Christianity in the world.

Without the apostolic anointing of God's Spirit, ministries are operating illegally and out of His planned order for the church.

When ministries say they are the arm of the church, and subvert the doctrine of Jesus Christ and disobey the commands of God they are deceivers. Just as Zerubbabel was able to discern the true motives of Shimshai, (Ezra 7:1), we must do the same by carefully analyzing what leaders say. It is clear in ministry today that some ministries have not found a place within the structure of God's plan to work. They are independent in spirit, belief and doctrine, but still want to be accepted by the body of Christ. They have seen the need in the body of Christ for restoration of God's order, but refuse not to obey and lead according to God's plan. Therefore, their ministries are operating without the spiritual authority of Jesus Christ. A ministry has spiritual authority because the leader has a revelation from the Lord.

If there is no revelation or vision within the parameters of God's order, the ministry of establishing and discipling is counterfeit. Authority can be created by leaders of strong willed personalities which cause ministries to not be legitimately recognized or established. This type of disregard for spiritual authority opens up the ministry for erroneous teaching and the misguidance of the people of God. People assume that all, or at least almost all, who bear the name Christian follow the beliefs, teachings and practices of Jesus Christ. But the Bible tells us that not everyone who accepts the name of Christ is really a Christian (Matthew 24:4-5). Jesus predicted that some would claim His name but would deny Him by their actions. He said they would "call Me 'Lord, Lord,'" but "not do the things which I say" (Luke 6:46).

Christ and His apostles spoke of false prophets, false apostles and false brethren. They revealed that two opposing ostensibly Christian religions would emerge. One, the Church Jesus founded would be led by God's Spirit and remain faithful to His teachings. The other will be guided and influenced by a different spirit, would accept the name of Christ but twist His teachings to create a convincing counterfeit of the truth. Both would use Christ's name and claim His authority. Both would perform works that would outwardly appear good and right. Both would claim to be following Christ's true teachings. But only one would faithfully represent its founder, Jesus Christ.

The other would capture the minds and hearts of humanity by attaching the name of Christ to biblically unsupportable religious customs and doctrines that Jesus and His apostles neither practiced nor approved. Believers should be conscience that the authority of the Lord alone should be maintained as expressed in His word. Even in apostolic days self-will entered in the case of Diotrephes. He was one who wanted to lead according to his own will, instead of God's will. He would shut apostolic order from the saints, looking on the people as his property (John 3).

Erroneous Doctrine

As the apostles strove to establish more congregations of believers, an alternate and outwardly Christian religion different from the order of God and what Jesus established arose. New and different doctrines were subtly introduced. Some began subverting the Church by challenging and contradicting the teachings of Christ's apostles. Paul warned, "For there are many insubordinate, both idle talkers and deceivers, especially those of the circumcision, whose mouths must be stopped, who subvert whole households, teaching things which ought not, for the sake of dishonest gain" (Titus 1:10-11). It doesn't take much to start a new movement, but to work and function within God's apostolic order we must obey the Spirit of God and His direction. Peter and the other apostles risked their lives to make it clear that "we ought to obey God rather than men" (Acts 5:29). Paul expressed the same commitment he shared with the other apostles – of a life of obedience. Paul later cautioned members of the church of Colosse to hold fast to what he had taught them. "As you have therefore received Christ Jesus the Lord, so walk in Him, rooted and built up in Him and established in the faith, as you have been taught (Colossians 2:8-9, 13).

Jude 3 speaks about "the faith" for which Christians are to contend. The term "faith" is used in essentially two senses, the personal, subjective faith of individuals and the gospel system (Rom. 14: 22, 23; Acts 13: 8). "The faith" (te pistei) very appropriately stands for the gospel system in view of the fact that the faith has the design and goal of producing personal faith in the individual (Rom. 10: 17, Jn. 20: 30, 31). Jude 3 is tantamount to

Paul's language, "...I am set for the defense of the gospel" (Phili. 1: 17). The gospel is more than just the death, burial, and resurrection of Jesus (these are the facts of the gospel, I Cor. 15: 1-4). The terms "the gospel" and "the faith" are used comprehensively to involve belief and consequent manner of life (cp. Gal. 2: 14).

There is skepticism among believers as well as nonbeliever concerning the teachings and practices of our churches today. A too often prevailing attitude seen in the religious world and even in the Lord's church is that of doctrinal indifference. "So what if they teach thus and so, what does it really matter?" is the statement often made to express this doctrinal tolerance. The real question should be, "how would God have us view the matter of doctrine and does the truth really matter?" To answer this question and to establish what our thinking should be relative to matters doctrine. As we observe these ministries and search the scriptures we realize that there are significant discrepancies between what is being taught and what God says in His Word. Jesus commanded His apostles to teach others exactly what He had taught –"teaching them to obey everything I have commanded you" (Matthew 28:20). He condemned the replacing of God's commandments with traditions and human reason. Speaking to the Pharisees, He said, "For laying aside the commandment of God, you hold the tradition of men ... All too well you reject the commandment of God, that you may keep your tradition" (Mark 7:8-9).

Traditions are very important in some religions, such as the Roman Catholic, and in the Protestant church. The Roman Catholic "tradition" is regarded as the Word of God.

> "It is an article of faith from a decree of the Vatican Council that Tradition is a source of theological teaching distinct from the Scripture, and that it is infallible. It is therefore to be received with the same internal assent of Scripture, for it is the Word of God." – Catholic Dictionary, p. 41-42.

"Do you believe in Tradition? Yes, because it is the Word of God and has equal authority with the Bible." Catholic Catechism For Adults, p. 11.

Just about every Protestant church has its own tradition and it is often these accepted teachings that distinguish between the denominations. To be a member of a particular denomination, you must accept its teachings. Jesus taught His church to keep the commandments of God. And like Jesus the apostles consistently taught obedience to God. Peter and the other apostles risked their lives to make it clear that "we ought to obey God rather than men" (Acts 5:29). Paul later cautioned members of the congregation in Colosse to hold fast to what he had taught them. Following Christ's example, Paul warned the Colosse not to accept traditions as replacements for the commandments of God. Jesus sounded urgent alarms warning us to avoid the traditions of men.

The Greek word for tradition is "paradosis", which means "giving over" or "handing down". It refers to teaching that which is handed down either by word of mouth or in writing. In Jewish custom, tradition is often applied to the oral teachings of the elders. These traditions were often divided into three classes; (a) some oral laws allegedly given by Moses in addition to the written laws; (b) decisions of various judges which became precedents in judicial matters; and (c) interpretations of highly respected rabbis which were held in reverence along with the Old Testament scriptures. (ISBE)

The word tradition that is found in the New Testament three times refers to apostolic teachings which had been delivered by the apostles. Christians were expected to keep these sayings. Ten times it refers to the tradition of the elders or the tradition of men of which Paul warned the Colossians and from which Jewish Christians had been delivered. Jesus did not feel bound to abide by the traditions of men. Some traditions He had no problem keeping such as, going to a wedding feast, attending a Feast of Dedication. But others like plucking a grain of wheat, healing on the Sabbath, or eating with unwashed hands were not a problem violating.

Jesus did not subscribe to the view of traditions handed down orally. He never appealed to the traditions of the elders because He is the Word of God in the flesh. He either appealed to the authority of the written Word (the Law of Moses), or to His own authority as the Son of God. Not all traditions are wrong. When they are teachings inspired of God, given and written by men approved by God, they are to be heeded. But when they are doctrines or interpretations handed down by uninspired men, to enslave, manipulate and control they are doctrines of men.

New and different doctrines are still being introduced today. Some are subverting the Church by challenging and contradicting the teachings of Christ's apostles. Paul warned, "For there are many insubordinate, both idle talkers and deceivers, especially those of the circumcision, whose mouths must be stopped, who subvert whole households, teaching things which they ought not, for the sake of dishonest gain" (Titus 1:10-11). To counter this trend, Paul instructed follow elder Titus to carefully consider the background, knowledge and character of anyone being considered for ordination.

The result of changing the doctrines has produced the scattering of the church by introducing teachings contrary to God's order and what we believe. Those changes altered the vision. It altered the vision of all of us, to some degree—making us split into many organizations—because certain things seemed more or less important to us individually. The changing of the doctrines caused us all to wander in Egypt for awhile, just as Abraham did. Egypt serves metaphorically as a "type" of the world. So, like Abraham, we have had to go back to a beginning (in order to make sure of our bearings) so then, hopefully, we can rapidly move on.

God clearly reveals a consistent, unchanging pattern in His word concerning His intender order. He delivers doctrine to the church through the highest-ranking representative of His government available at the time. In the Bible, the representative might be "a prophet," "an apostle," "an ambassador," "a messenger," or "a preacher." It doesn't matter which—the title of the Spirit filled believer is less important than the office held.

Now under the Old Covenant the office used was that of a prophet. Under the New Covenant it was apostle, and God consistently communicated His will and order, His doctrines, His teachings, His pleasures, through those offices. Beginning with Abel, God names those men. And when we get to the New Testament church, it was clearly Peter who was first among equals. Then, as the responsibility of the office that Peter held became too great (considering the times and the lack of technology that they had), God divided that office between Peter and Paul. So the thrust of Peter's ministry from that time on was solely to the Israelites, and Paul's to the Gentiles.

So God established the doctrines that specified His order for His end time church according to the same patterns that He always used in the past so that we might have faith in an unchanging God. God doesn't shift gears in the middle of something, throwing us into confusion, because what God wants to lead us to is not merely believing something intellectually, but actively trusting Him through our application of those doctrines. So He did this through the apostle and only one was needed (rather than the number that was given to the New Testament first century church) because of the technology available today. Now those doctrines given through him are to be the base of our faith and our operations. Paul wrote II Thessalonians 2:15 to a congregation that was having some problems. They were having problems with division and disorderliness (II Thessalonians 2:15).

Increasingly, "false apostles" began contradicting and undermining the teachings of the true apostles of Christ. Paul cautioned the church in Rome to keep an eye on those who cause dissensions and offenses, in opposition to the teaching that they had learned. Competing religious leaders masquerading as ministers of Christ, began teaching their own false doctrines "in opposition to" Christ's apostles and other of his faithful servants. At first they came predominantly from a Jewish background. But then false teachers emerged from people of other backgrounds within the Church. The subversive doctrines that eventually grew to be the most influential were a blend of pagan and misguided Jewish philosophies synthesized with the mysticism popular at that time.

The impact of distorted teachings devastated the early Church. If we are not rooted and grounded in the Word of God we will believe a different gospel. Christians in the Roman province of Galatia turned en masse from the teachings of the apostle Paul to a corrupted, cunningly devised but counterfeit gospel promoted by false apostles. Different doctrines such as the Word of Faith, Healing, Prosperity, Holiness, Keeping the Sabbath, and so on have divided the body of Christ and tried to diminish the power of the Gospel of Jesus Christ. Salvation, or *soterion* is holistic in its' meaning encompasses and includes faith, deliverance, healing, prosperity, and holiness. We as leaders are to preach the Kingdom of God and His righteousness and all these things shall be added unto us.

Many Christians are being swept into one of many sects making up the emerging false Christianity. What is curious to me is the humanistic approach envisioning themselves to be little gods. This is so outrageous, because if I had anything to do with creation it would be a real mess. Paul had to contend with the strife, as we do today, generated by legalists, and teachers of false doctrines. These pretenders are so cunning. They know how to mix the gospel with their beliefs so you would think they did not reject the gospel. These false prophets and teachers have perverted aspects of the gospel. Then they seduce people into accepting their gospel of truth and error. It contains enough truth to appear righteous and Christian, but it has sufficient error to prevent any who would accept it from receiving Salvation.

Regard for God's commandments in mainstream Christianity has been remarkably inconsistent since the Protestant Reformation. On one hand, the Ten Commandments have been considered the greatest moral law mankind has ever known. On the other hand, they have usually been regarded as too inconsequential or arbitrary to be obligatory. These contradictory views of God's order concerning His church became evident in the 16th century with the theological differences between Martin Luther and John Calvin, the principal founders of Protestant theology.

Calvin believed Christians should keep the Ten Commandments. Calvin's view, though popular in past centuries, steadily lost ground during the 20th century. Today most Christian denominations reflect, at least in practice, Luther's view toward the commandments of God. Luther incorrectly assumed that the apostle Paul had rejected the authority of the Old Testament just as Luther had rejected the authority of the Catholic hierarchy of his day. Luther saw that Paul taught salvation by grace through faith (Ephesians 2:8).

By the end of the third century, it seemed the true servants of God had become a distinct minority among those who called themselves Christians. The counterfeit Christianity had become the majority. False teachers had successfully gained a far larger following than the faithful ministers of God. However, history shows the counterfeit sects were not united in their beliefs. Many factions existed among them. Nevertheless, divided and unconverted as it was, this new brand of Christianity rapidly expanded its membership and became the visible Christian church. Purporting to offer salvation, but without the necessity of real repentance, it held just enough truth to appeal to the masses. This counterfeit Christianity became a squabbling, bitterly divided religion.

But at the beginning of the fourth century two things happened that abruptly altered the course of Christian history. First, the Roman emperor Diocletian intensified the policy of many previous Roman emperors of persecuting Christians and ordered that all Christian manuscripts be burned. This dramatically renewed a climate of fear throughout the Christian community. Ten years later another emperor, Constantine, came to power. He had defeated another powerful contender for the right to replace Diocletian as emperor, but he still had many enemies, and his political position remained insecure. Constantine legalized Christianity. Two years later, he called all the divided professing Christian groups to hammer out a unified system of belief. He wanted a united religious body that was politically committed to him.

Many of our religious leaders today have sadly led many Christians astray. To avoid being misled we need to listen to them carefully, and pay close attention to the things they are teaching. We must first give all leaders, and teachers a fair and careful hearing by seeking to understand exactly what they are saying by being a good listener. Many are misled because they have never learned to listen carefully to what is being said and taught. We must search the scriptures daily by comparing what the teacher or leader says to the scriptures.

God has not called one man to be His authority in any ministry, nor has He called a group of men to be His authority in the church. He has called men who will allow His authority to flow through them. God's purpose shall be done and God's people will be cared for by God through men who are under authority. A man who is not submitted to the authority of God's order, has no authority and is not controlled by the Spirit of God. For the Church to function as the apostolic order of God, spiritual authority must be recognized and submitted to. God has not given His authority to just anyone or any ministry.

What is disturbing today is that man's direction is taking the place of the will of God and His intended order. For believers to do God's will they must know who God is and what He is doing by His Spirit. The believer must be spiritual to discern the revelations of what God who is a Spirit. If we were more spiritual and less carnal we would not believe in the many other things being done in the name of Jesus. What I mean by being spiritual is not speaking in tongues continuously, or being pious and overly judgmental, but being filled with the Spirit of God to know the things of God, and not be deceived by false doctrines. To know and understand the heart of God, we must develop the mind of Christ given us by His Holy Spirit. The mind of Christ consists of these virtues as described in Isaiah 11:2, and is drawn from the Spirit of the Lord, which produces wisdom, understanding, knowledge, counsel, might, and the fear of the Lord.

The reason there are so many different works in ministries, is the discovery of the need for the development of people to usher them into their purpose. Christians are feeling incomplete in regards to their service and walk with God. There is a void and an emptiness within them that seeks to be filled with the power of God. They desire to be validated in the realization that they are in the perfect will of God and God is pleased with them. Christians are seeking to be nurtured as well as mentored. Many Christians have been forced to function as disgruntle believers out of spiritual authority and God's order. This has caused separation and paranoia within the body and has led to the creation of their own doctrine and tradition.

Eli abandoned authority to his sons and did not restrain them when they made themselves vile (1 Sam. 3:13). It is so often that relatives of leaders are allowed to usurp their place and authority over a congregation of believers. When relatives who are not ordained by God to work in a given capacity occupy a position of rule, it violates God's order and introduces confusion and disorder. As the criteria for leadership changes, people begin to trust in the faith of their founder totally disregarding the apostolic order of God. The traditions may be different, but the people's faith in the tradition is just the same. In addition, this group or denomination often classifies themselves a certain way with a label they wear proudly as they befriend their tradition and defend it with an ethnic pride.

When people in a parent church are threatened by a new experience of others, opposition often begins to arise. Those people in the parent church who have put faith in their religious tradition often persecute and oppose them. The Catholic church excommunicated Martin Luther because he taught another gospel. In more recent history, many experiencing the baptism of the Holy Spirit during the outpouring at the Azusa Street Mission in Los Angeles in the early 1900s were asked to leave their churches.

When the new group is persecuted another thing occurs. Often a "martyr mentally" inflicts the group. Perceiving themselves to be victims, the people then grasp fiercely onto their spiritual experience and make a denomination or another group based on that doctrine or experience. Rapid growth may still continue, but the gospel continues to be spread in the spirit of that experience whether it is disgruntle, bitter or in error.

The world tends to reject any governmental direction or order from God. As believers who have received Jesus as they personal Savior and God and His laws as "our" way—or more accurately are filled with the Spirit of God—we begin to respond to Him. The point is, we are becoming one with Him and therefore rebel less as we grow into oneness. *His* government is one thing. *Church* government is a completely different thing! There is a definite difference between the government of God *by* God and a church government of men learning to govern as God Himself governs. No two men will do it exactly as Christ would. There are different administrations (I Corinthians 12:5, KJV). God accepts this as long as the leaders do not compromise the principles of His law.

CHAPTER XII.
GOD'S MANDATE FOR APOSTOLIC ORDER

The Church is the tool in the hand of God to accomplish His purpose in the earth. The Church is to be equipped by the five-fold ministry gifts. Understanding of the function of these gifts and making room for their operation in the Body of Christ brings maturity. The present move of the apostolic and prophetic ministry is a dispensational ministry to usher in the reign of the King and the establishment of His Kingdom. The restoration of the apostolic and prophetic ministry, as well as the pastors, evangelists and teachers are a means to the end.

According to **Ephesians 5:13**, the five-fold ministry gifts to the Church is an *"until ministry* . The principle focus is on the Kingdom. **Thy Kingdom come, thy will be done here on earth, as it is in heaven (Mathew 6:10).**

What is known as the church age has been characterized by human effort, traditions, programs and projects that has substituted the original plan and purposes of God, and this has been the result of we taking over God s Church and seek to run it our own ways. The Lord is demanding back His Church and we need to build according to the pattern and desire of God. *Church is not about us, our needs and desires, but is about God, His will and His desires.* God is restoring the Church to her original and essential role. The role of the Church is to fulfill the purpose of God in the earth as an agent that will finish and reach the goal of God. The purpose of the Church is the Kingdom, and without the Kingdom the Church has no purpose; likewise the purposes of the Kingdom will not be fulfilled without the Church. The Church is becoming the mystery of the ages that will stand and overcome.

Some leaders today, are operating illegally and without an apostolic anointing. Having an apostolic anointing requires a potential leader to stay under leadership that has been bestowed with an apostolic prophetic anointing. Sometimes when you are under leadership that has either a prophetic or an apostolic anointing the Holy Spirit will supply the anointing needed for ministry. In other words the Holy Spirit will allow you to experience an apostolic prophetic mantle that will cause you to investigate how to obtain this type of anointing.

The Message: God's passion is to recover and restore His Kingdom in the earth yet the Church lacks understanding of the message. The Church has proclaimed the gospel of salvation with a focus on getting the people to heaven rather than bringing heaven to earth. The message is key to accomplish God s purpose (**see Luke 4:42-43 and Revelation 11:15).** *The mandate of the Church is to preach the message (gospel) of the Kingdom for a witness in the world and then the end shall come* **(Matthew 25:14).** The responsibility of the great commission is an apostolic charge. Apostolic strategies will be revealed and implemented. These will produce God's order in the Church and establish the Kingdom of God in the earth.

After His ascension, the Lord Jesus Christ gave specific gifts to men to accomplish a specific mission. These gifts given to men are generally referred to as the five-fold ministry gifts. The five-fold ministry gifts are tools in the process of Kingdom order and the fulfillment of God s purpose.

The present apostolic order equips the Church with knowledge and understanding of both the *order of ministry* and the *order of government* . The fivefold ministry gifts of apostles, prophets, teachers, pastors and evangelist will be released and become operational.

All five-fold ministry gifts can plant a local assembly where the Church meets. Apostles and prophets lay the foundations. All five-fold ministries possess the characteristics of eldership and may exercise administrative and spiritual oversight. The saints are matured when the five offices operate in a local church.

As apostolic order is established, the Church can progress into maturity and perfection. God intended that the drive towards perfection is the goal of the Church. God has ordained the five-fold ministry gifts to bring the Church into maturity and perfection by the word of God and His Spirit. Without the authority and ministry of the apostles, prophets, teachers, pastors and evangelists the Church would be unstable and immature. However, the Church is moving towards maturity as the five-fold ministry gifts function. These gifts will continue to operate in the Church *until* God s purpose is accomplished.

The Church is the operation of the Body of Christ in a locality coming together with a singular vision and purpose for the Kingdom of God to advance and be established. This is not a denominational form of structure, but it is a work of the Holy Spirit in the hearts of the people to model the 5-Fold Ministry in the New Testament where there is no divisions and lack, but all continued in the apostles doctrine, breaking of bread, fellowshipping together, praying and worshipping God without any interior motives of personal gain. The Church establishes an apostolic community where its influence and scope is according to Kingdom principles.

Today s church was the temple in the book of Acts and the Acts Church referred to the Christians, the followers of Christ. We need to define the terms as we present our gospel to prevent offence and opposition to the apostolic order. The apostolic order of God does include the in the Church. *Apostolic order does not oppose the Church, but rather calls for a return to the New Testament pattern of apostolic structures in fulfilling the purpose of God in the earth.* To this end, a need to come out from *some* of the present Babylonian church systems and religious denominations is recognized.

The Children of Israel in the Old Testament were the ekklesia that represented the Church in that order **(Acts 7:38)**. One of the goals of God is that the Church would be the instrument to establish His Kingdom on the earth. *The churches are not the Kingdom of God, but they represent the Kingdom as ambassadors* *upon the earth, and aim to establish a heavenly colony of the Kingdom of God.* The Old Testament ekklesia (Church) had a functional preparatory of establishing the Kingdom of God in the earth. As called out ones from Egypt, the desire of God was to separate them as unique ones to represent His Kingdom and demonstrate His life and character to distinguish them from all other nations and kingdoms.

Moses received an instruction that the Children of Israel were to build God a sanctuary (house, haven) that He might dwell amongst them. God s desire from the beginning of the ages is to find a shelter, a dwelling among men upon the earth. **.let them make me a sanctuary: that I may dwell among them. According to all that I shew thee, after the pattern of the tabernacle, and the pattern of all the instruments thereof, even so shall ye make it. (Exodus 25:8-9).** In this present day, the Lord has moved from dwelling in tents and He now tabernacles Himself in men - the Church - as His permanent house here on earth. We have become the temple of the Lord in which He resides. No longer is God content to visit, He seeks to abide permanently. We must go beyond the visitation experience. God wants to live in His house!

Much today does not indicate order in the house of God. There is displacement and dislocation as everyone is seeking his own way. Few are seeking the Lord for a clear word. As a result, frustrated leaders and churches are running to and fro, attending conferences for new church growth techniques. All that is received is another man s vision, methods and principles that does not work for them. I am not saying that the principles are not of God. They are the revelation of God s word given to His Church in a particular geographical location for that time and purpose. These principles and methods were given by God to men for their church, city and nation. We are not obligated to carry this to our own church, city or nation. It is not a mandatory pattern and method for all churches and leaders in other nations. The personal word of revelation from the Lord for each church, city and nation is the key to successful Church growth.

Christ and His Church is a corporate Body (a many member Body). The Church of Jesus Christ is not a religious organization. It is an organism. It is the community of a faith and the people of a Kingdom. The Church indeed is the people of the Kingdom of God, but the visible *church* is not the Kingdom. *The Church has never been a denomination or a building raised up somewhere in the city or nation, but it is a realm of God s Kingdom community that is embodied within a people that have been called out.*

Let me clearly emphasize here that I am not trying to rule out the importance of the Church as she has a role to play that is very vital to the purposes of God. **Without the Church the Kingdom of God cannot be established and likewise without the Kingdom the Church has no purpose.** The Kingdom of God is and must be the motivation for the Church. All that the Church is made for is to reflect the Kingdom of God in the earth.

We need to understand what the Church is. Church is not the physical structures and buildings nor is it the sum of all its organizations. It is a higher sense of peoplehood than most of us think. The Church is a corporate member Body of people that is greater than the churches and denominations. Just as the Israel of God s purpose (the remnant saved by grace) is not the same as the Israelite nation **(Romans 1:1-5, Romans 2:28-29, Romans 9:6-8, Galatians 6:16),** neither person nor assembly can claim to be the One True Church .

The One True Church is the corporate community of all who have heard the sound of the Kingdom of God and have responded by faith and submitted themselves to His reign and rule through obedience, saying yes to His Kingdom. This makes the Church a universal community. The early Church is the successor of the Israel of God s purpose in the Old Testament and the true remnant and people in the New Testament (New Covenant) chosen by His grace with a primary mandate and mission of proclaiming the Kingdom and extending the covenant of God to the nations. The Church is called to embody the righteousness of God s Kingdom and mandated with proclaiming that Kingdom in all nations. *The goal of the Church is not to establish herself upon the earth as we see today through our programs and developments, but the primary purpose of the Church is to establish the Kingdom of God. The Church cannot be matured and established without the establishment of God s Kingdom through the ministry of* **Ephesians 4:11**.

God s Kingdom is supreme over earthly order and authority. The Church is the people of the Kingdom; therefore the Church is to become the ultimate authority and government in the earth. The goal and purpose of transition into an apostolic culture must be shared with the people, so that the core ideology, values, principles and plan of God for the Church will be clearly articulated and they can understand the new season and revelation of God they are coming into. From these ideals will come the philosophy that will accurately epitomize and characterize the values, goals and attitudes of the Kingdom in that local assembly. The result will be a successful transition and a complete change into the new season of God.

Accurate Kingdom culture and the way of life and perspective are not operational within the old existing religious church patterns and systems. The process of transition will bring a structural adjustment in the mindsets of the people and this will need an impartation from authentic apostolic and prophetic leaders to assist the Church make a successfully transition, lest we will fail and bring a total destruction of the process that will affect the church. To receive the authentic and refuse the false, each local assembly must be taught about apostolic and prophetic ministries, as well as the other five-fold ministry gifts, because many are out there parading and claiming apostleship.

Antioch churches are local churches with apostolic kingdom perspective. These churches have a dynamic vision of sending out apostolic teams to reproduce apostolic churches in other territories and nations in order to advance the Kingdom of God. They are modeled on the apostolic Church that was in Antioch as mentioned in **Acts 13**.

New Testament churches must become prototype Antioch churches that have a sending spirit. The sending spirit of the Antioch church can be birthed in the local
church, changing it from a camping ground to a training and dispatch centre. Those who are trained must be released into the

work. The apostolic spirit is a sending spirit whose hallmark is the conveyance of grace.

In the church at Antioch there were these prophets and teachers: Barnabas, Simeon (also called Niger), Lucius (from the city of Cyrene), Manaen (who had grown up with Herod, the ruler), and Saul. They were all worshiping the Lord and giving up eating (fasting) for a certain time. During this time the Holy Spirit said to them, "Set apart for me Barnabas and Saul to do a special work for which I have chosen them."So after they gave up eating (fasting) and prayed, they laid their hands on Barnabas and Saul and sent them out. Barnabas and Saul, sent out by the Holy Spirit, went to the city of Seleucia. From there they sailed to the island of Cyprus. (Acts 13:1-4 - New Century Translation).

Antioch Churches are proto-type New Testament patterned apostolic company with a sending mentality to release others into the work of the ministry under the specific direction of the Holy Spirit. They are apostolic **[Greek: apostello]** in nature, a company of saints called out and sent forth to declare the Kingdom of God in the earth under the oversight of apostolic leadership and the direction of the Holy Spirit. They are a sent company.

The character of a true Antioch apostolic Church is that it has an apostolic measure and dimension of grace. It is that of the five-fold ministry gifts in operation. It is very prophetic in nature, it is an evangelically oriented Church, and it provides pastoral function and a proper discipleship value for teaching the people in other to produce matured saints.

There must be an alignment in leadership pattern – (the five-fold ministry must be fully embraced and set in order to function in God's intended order). We are in a transitional season that requires the local church to redefine and plan for transition into Kingdom dynamics of a five-fold ministry model of operation. There is such a great level of apathy and immaturity in the church because tradition customs and rituals, we have not fully recognized and received the Apostolic order of the five-fold ministry that the Lord has given to us.

The result of this negligence has resulted in not appropriating the full benefits of the cross, absence of unity and ignorance of the purposes of God. The fact remains that if we are ignorant of the primary purposes of God and continue to minister and build in the old pattern, we will miss Gods order bringing Kingdom of God on earth as it is in Heaven and be in error. We must move beyond our pastoral priority to an active involvement in bringing the God's apostolic order, a work that is beyond the activities of the local assembly in building the house of God and establishing His Kingdom on earth.

Kingdom churches are territorial churches. They are strategically positioned to be gate keepers in the city. They keep watch over activities in the region. They have governmental authority at their disposal to enforce Kingdom purposes. Apostolic ordered churches are governmental churches that have a Kingdom perspective with the ability to impact and influence their region and the earth as agents of change. We must become a spiritual government and a pattern in our region. This is clearly seen in the expression of the Antioch church because the disciples were first called Christians in Antioch (Acts 11:26).

Antioch was a discipleship training center for believers to be developed, equipped and released. In Antioch these believers who became disciples were called Christians. It was not the Lord that called the disciples Christians, neither was it the apostles, but it was the world that called them Christians because of the expression of their faith and lifestyle that was having an influence in the community and beyond. As an Apostolic God order patterned church, we must be strategically positioned in a region to invade the market-place community and economic Babylon to plunder it for the Kingdom of God.

CHAPTER XIII:
KINGDOM APOSTOLIC ORDER

Today's church was the temple in the book of Acts and the Acts Church referred to the Christians, the followers of Christ. We need to define the terms as we present our gospel to prevent offence and opposition to the apostolic order. The apostolic transitioning does believe in the Church. *The apostolic Spirit does not oppose the Church, but rather calls for a return to the New Testament pattern of apostolic structures in fulfilling the purpose of God in the earth.* To this end, a need to come out from *some* of the present Babylonian church systems and religious Denominations is recognized.

One of the goals of God is that the Church would be the instrument to establish His Kingdom on the earth. *The churches are not the Kingdom of God, but they represent the Kingdom as ambassadors upon the earth, and aim to establish a heavenly colony of the Kingdom of God.* The Old Testament ekklesia (Church) had a functional preparatory of establishing the Kingdom of God in the earth. As called out ones from Egypt, the desire of God was to separate them as unique ones to represent His Kingdom and demonstrate His life and character to distinguish them from all other nations and kingdoms.

In this present day the Church is a nation **ethnos a race, a tribe** of people who are scattered abroad, but are bound by the same Kingdom and governmental laws, principles and culture under the Lordship and leadership of Jesus Christ. The purpose of the Church in the earth is to administer the government of God s

Apostolic Kingdom Order. Those called out by God s grace into God s ekklesia family are called, not merely for salvation and eternal life, but to learn the ways of God and His Kingdom and to develop His divine character upon the earth. The objective of the Church is to take responsibility to declare the gospel of the Kingdom of God. This act will bring restoration of God s heavenly government on the earth and the ousting of Satan s rule over the people. The intent and desire of God is to apostolically order the earth and bring all things under subjection through the Church for the return of Jesus Christ **(Psalm 110:1-2, Romans 16:20).**

> The Church will manifest the unsearchable riches of Christ.
> The Church will make known the manifold wisdom of God unto principalities and powers in heavenly places, according to the eternal purpose that God prepared in Christ Jesus before the foundation of the world.

The Lord will not inhabit an unfinished building; neither will His glory come down
on an unfinished house. For this reason;

> The Church has not yet experienced the fullness of God s glory that will be greater than the former.
> The Church will reveal the excellency of the glory of God. To do so we must remove every hindrance, veil, darkness of ignorance, spiritual blindness, dishonesty, craftiness and deceitfulness.

God s intent in dwelling among us is to manifest His great and excellent glory. It is for the builder and the house to bear the glory **(Zachariah 6:13).**

> Tradition is any religious practice, statement, precept, legend, custom, belief, system or teaching handed down from one generation to the other by the words of our mouth or by practice that replaces the revelation of the Spirit of God. Tradition is developed to replace the word of God when the people lost focus of what the Lord is saying and where He is. It is easy to lose focus on God and become busy with religious activities and programs thinking that God is in it, and He is not. Pharisees are agents who promote traditions **(Mark 7:3).** *In the Church today, the manifestation of a Pharisee spirit is visible when God begins to move the Church into a new dimension of spiritual truth and to*

change the order and structure of existing revelation in the Body of Christ.

The Pharisee spirit in a passive and flaccid. The traditional church holds to the voice of the past moves and rejects the present voice and truth. A spirit of rebellion manifests as stubbornness and unwillingness to yield to the present move of God in the earth. Leaders, board members, elders, deacons and decision makers are at risk of deception through lack of understanding and revelation of the Holy Spirit regarding the actions of God. This gives place for the spirit of Jezebel to enter and begin to rule and oversee the activities of the Church.

The dynamic change occurring in the Body brings about an apostolic order of reconfiguration for the establishment of pragmatic truths in the Church. It is the release of present truths . There are past truths and present truths . If we are to come into the new things that God is doing, we need to leave behind past truths and come into the new day and season of God where present truths are released. *The Church must be established in present truth.* We have gone too far from true biblical order, truths and teachings and we have sought to establish our own traditional ecclesiastical order. This has affected the corporate Body and hinders the revelations of the purposes of God in the earth. One of the enemies and hindrances in seeing an apostolic order and reformation is the tradition of men and denominational doctrines that have been set in place. We need to begin to do things God s way. *The pursuit of truth is the noblest responsibility that we have during this reformation season.* As people of God's Apostolic order, we must become purposely placed in God's word and become spiritually balanced.

Establishment of foundation is essential to the building of God s house. The foundation of the God's apostolic order is being restructured and restored. This activates the apostolic mandate to establish the Kingdom of God in the earth. Established apostolic structure and function will train, equip and release the Church to fulfill God s purpose in the earth. It is important to note here that the apostolic and prophetic foundation is nothing of self-ministry, but it is simply the establishing of Christ as the Foundation in the local Church through and effective teaching and impartation of the revelation of Jesus for proper building of God s Kingdom of the

Father's house. The place of completion and perfection awaits the Body of Christ. To understand the mysteries of the Kingdom of God the Church must lay aside elementary doctrine. Maturity of the Church through the operation of the five-fold ministry gifts will enable the Body to complete the purposes of God in the earth.

The apostles' doctrine is the foundational teaching of Jesus Christ. Foundational doctrines are uncovered from revelation of the apostles' doctrine. To be established in foundational doctrine is to receive the fullness of the apostles' doctrine that is to ground the Church in the principles of Jesus teaching. Outside this foundational doctrine of Jesus Christ, the Church cannot attain perfection. As apostolic order is established, the Church can progress into maturity and perfection. God intended that the drive towards perfection is the goal of the Church. God has ordained the five-fold ministry gifts to bring the Church into maturity and perfection by the word of God and His Spirit. Without the authority and ministry of the apostles, prophets, teachers, pastors and evangelists the Church would be unstable and immature. However, the Church is moving towards maturity as the
five-fold ministry gifts function. These gifts will continue to operate in the Church *until* God s purpose is accomplished.

The Church must embrace the apostolic order of God, evaluate present truths, and transition with the move of the Spirit to fulfill God s purpose in the earth.

The Urban Church is the operation of the Body of Christ with a mandate of God's apostolic order, in a locality. Their coming together is with a singular vision and purpose for the Kingdom of God to advance and be established. This unity is not a denominational form of structure, but it is a work of the Holy Spirit in the hearts of the people to model God's original intent in the New Testament where there is no divisions and lack, but all continued in the apostles' doctrine, breaking of bread, fellowshipping together, praying and worshipping God without any interior motives of personal gain.

God is beginning to redefine His Church in this new season to align with His purpose. As this shift from the traditional local church will result. *The unfolding of God s purpose is determined by times and seasons, and is initiated by new revelations from God.*

The Church has come into a new day and season in God. Progressively, God is showing us His original pattern and making us to understand His plan. He is showing us how far things have moved away from His plan and is revealing the process of restoration that is to align us to His purposes. We must accurately align our lives and ministries to God s ways and purpose. Like the sons of Issachar, we must be wise and have understanding of the times and seasons of God so we can then position ourselves to know what we ought to do and be in tune with Him and His moves.

An unknown author once said, Everything God has created goes through a transition easily and expectantly except man. Creation responds to a preordained command and renders its faithfulness simply because it *is the season.* Nature experiences change as a normal part of life, but we who actually have understanding of the importance of change, have great difficulty in allowing the transition to become a finished work not recognizing the significance of each season as an integral part in the process of maturing in God and being current in His present move. The Church is in a season of progression, progression into the fullness and purpose of God. It is impossible to live and operate in an old system and expect to soar in a new dimension, unless we respond to God s change in us. Only God is able to give wings to our purpose, so we can rise up as new and soar to the heights of glory in Him.

The present Godly intended Kingdom Apostolic order requires change in the Body of Christ to align to the true and authentic purposes of God. The required change is a migration from a pastoral mentality to an apostolic dimension, teachings and doctrines . It is important to recognize that the Church is not about us but is about God and His purpose. On that basis, we can allow God to work in and through us as He begins to perfect things in us. Authentic apostolic ordered ministry brings a dynamic of mindset change to receive that which God is declaring now concerning His Kingdom purpose. It is the duty of every leader to find and walk in their true calling. This requires that leaders must migrate towards a

God intentional apostolic paradigm of ministry in order to bring blessing and establishment to the Church.

Congregations have been taught and foundations have been built upon certain eschatological theories, theories proven wrong when authentic based God intended apostolic and prophetic theology and declarations are brought forth. What can be said to the congregation? Flexibility and humility are required to approach the matter and wisely present it to the Church. It is right to stand before the people to declare that we were wrong, although at the time we thought it to be the truth.

The goal and purpose of dynamic change into a God intended apostolic culture must be shared with the people, so that the core ideology, values, principles and plan of God for the Church will be clearly articulated and they can understand the new season and revelation of God they are coming into. From these ideals will come the philosophy that will accurately epitomize and characterize the values, goals and attitudes of the Kingdom in that local assembly. The result will be a successful transition and a complete change into the new season of God.

Accurate Godly kingdom apostolic culture and the dynamic way of thinking and perspective are not operational within the old existing religious church patterns and systems. The process of transition will bring a structural adjustment in the mindsets of the people and this will need an impartation from authentic apostolic and prophetic leaders to assist the Church make a successful transition, lest we will fail and bring total destruction of the process that will affect the church. To receive the authentic and refuse the false, each local assembly must be taught about the five-fold ministry gifts, because many are out there parading and claiming apostleship.

Leaders can delay and hinder the transition of the people for a season, but they will eventually come to the knowledge of truth and the confrontation may be greater as a result. As we make the transition from pastoral priorities to apostolic order, the local Church must realign to walk in an apostolic mentality and measurement capable of advancing the sovereignty of God in the earth. The entire framework and perspective of the kingdom apostolic change and order is based upon the principle of Jesus' teachings and alignment.

Graham Cook states in his book, **A Divine Confrontation:**

"In transition we will need friends from outside who can provide objective support and care. We also need access to people who understand transition and process. In transition, we are re-digging the foundation of the Church so that the Lord can erect a bigger building and release a greater dynamic of corporate power and identity. The only people who can really help us now are apostles and prophets. They are foundational ministers. It is inevitable in transition that our structures are going to change. New paradigms need to form as God delivers us from being stereotype to a prototype Church. Changes must come. We need prophetic insight and apostolic strategy combining together to redevelop the foundation and structure of the work by teaching, advice, prophecy and impartation they can furnish the building blocks to enable us to bridge the gap between where we are now and where we aspire to be."

The Church cannot go beyond where the leaders take them. As leaders, we cannot give that which we do not possess. We cannot take the people of God beyond our present level where we are. This places a demand upon each leader to continually progress and upgrade in technology so we can lead the people of God into new and higher levels. This also requires transparency and freedom from greed and spiritual abuse of God s gifts and people as they submit to leadership authority.

Antioch Churches are proto-type New Testament patterned apostolic company with a sending nature to release others into the work of the ministry under the specific direction of the Holy Spirit. They are apostolic **[Greek: apostello]** in nature, a company of saints called out and sent forth to declare the Kingdom of God in the earth under the oversight of apostolic leadership and the direction of the Holy Spirit. They are a sent company.

The character of a true Godly kingdom apostolic ordered Church is that it has an apostolic measure and dimension of grace. It is that of the five-fold ministry gifts are in operation. It is very prophetic in nature, it is an evangelically oriented Church, and it provides pastoral function and a proper discipleship value for teaching the people in other to produce matured saints

God ordered kingdom apostolic Churches are those that have moved beyond the limitations of culture and race. They are multi-cultural and multi-racial as this is expressed in leadership. Both Jews and Gentiles shared leadership responsibility over the Church and they reached both communities. Lucius who was part of the 5 men in leadership, was a black man from Libya in Africa. This applies to Simeon who was called Niger and was also a proselyte from Africa. There was no discrimination. The Antioch church differs from the Jerusalem church which had ethnic limitations because they ministered only to the Jews. Today we are reminiscent of the Jerusalem Church, having divided the church with racism, nepotism, our traditions, our doctrines and denominational barriers. This can be clearly seen in churches that have become tribalistic and racial, as black and white leaders encourage and lead those of the same color who become predominant in the midst of others. God is calling for a unified body of all races and nations to fulfill His purpose. The pigmentations of our skins should not be an issue, but our hearts.

There must be an alignment in leadership pattern – (the five-fold ministry must be fully embraced and set in order to function freely). We are in a transitional season that requires the local church to shift into a five-fold ministry model of operation. We have spoken much about this, but the application of the principles has been slow and the characters have not been fully formed. The reason why there is such a great level of immaturity in the church is because we have not fully recognized and received the five-fold ministry that the Lord has given to us. The result of this negligence has resulted to immaturity, absence of unity and ignorance of the purposes of God. The fact remains that if we are ignorant of the primary purposes of God and continue to minister and build in the old pattern, we will go into error. We must move beyond our pastoral priority to an active involvement in the apostolic work, a work that is beyond the activities of the local assembly in building the house of God and establishing His Kingdom on earth.

Our church must mirror the Antioch pattern that was characterized by their giving to God. They were generous in sending relief to the brethren in Judea by the hands of Barnabas and Saul. They did this according to their ability in response to the prophetic ministry that signified that there should be a great dearth throughout the entire world: which came to pass in the days of Claudius Caesar (Acts 11:27-30). Every local church must adopt this principle and abound in the grace of giving. There is no church that has nothing to give. If we have a vision for the establishment of an Antioch church, then our provision will be greatly determined by this grace. The measure of our vision determines the measure of God's provision to us.

The church must be a strong Godly apostolic ministry that ministers to God (Acts 13:2). The kingdom apostolic ministry is a primary focus of our assignment in the earth. It is first about our devotion to God before our service to the people. The effectiveness of our ministry to the people is a result of our commitment to minister *first* to God. The priestly ministry is *first* our devotion to God which is expressed in our prayers, worship and intercession. This is the secret of hearing the voice of God and walking in obedience to His divine instruction.

Antioch churches are territorial churches. They are strategically positioned to be gate keepers in the city. They keep watch over activities in the region. They have governmental authority at their disposal to enforce Kingdom purposes. Apostolic churches are governmental churches that have a Kingdom perspective with the ability to impact and influence their region and the earth as agents of change. We must become a spiritual government and a pattern in our region. This is clearly seen in the expression of the Antioch church because the disciples were first called Christians in Antioch (Acts 11:26). Antioch was a discipleship training center for believers to be developed, equipped and released. In Antioch these believers who became disciples were called Christians. It was not the Lord that called the disciples Christians, neither was it the apostles, but it was the world that called them Christians because of the expression of their faith and lifestyle that was having an influence in the community and beyond. As an Antioch patterned church, we must be strategically positioned in a region to invade the market-place community and economic Babylon to plunder it for the Kingdom of God.

The desire of God is to raise a prototype of an Antioch church that has significantly changed its status quo to affect the old system. There must be a new work that is established or restructured in the region, after the pattern of an Antioch church that is governmental, to impact and influence cities and nations for the Kingdom of God. These churches will become governmental churches that are local ministries with a global vision that seeks to reach beyond. The present faith level of the church must increase to a measure of influence, a measure to reach beyond. As well as being a local church family like the Jerusalem church, we should also have a worldwide vision like the Antioch church.

The apostolic church is a Kingdom church that was built apostolically that carried the gospel message of the Kingdom to regions beyond, because it was apostolic by birth, vision and function. If our present day church is not kingdom, then it is not apostolic, because the goal and message of the apostolic is the kingdom (Matthew 10:1-7). We must also send out apostolic fivefold ministry teams to reach the nations. This is a pattern of an Antioch church. Presently God is releasing "heavenly patterns" for establishing His church in the earth that will manifest His Kingdom and sovereignty like the Antioch church. There is a need for us to reform.

Dynamics of Transitioning into God Intended Apostolic Order

In every move of God the structures and patterns of the Church change. The term structures involve many aspects of Church life and activity. The nature of our prayer changes from constant requests for survival to powerful declaration of our intention to overcome and finish the work of the Lord. We call this Governmental Prayer. The nature of relationships between saints in the Kingdom changes as we move to purer positions of covenant as our sight of the Lord becomes clearer. Our attitude to financial matters changes, as we become more Kingdom minded and less selfish in that area of the ministry. In fact, all the activities of people that constitute a community of the Lord: a "church" begin to be adjusted by the changing winds of the Spirit. A move of God inevitably involves profound changes taking place within the structure of the Church (Luke 5: 37,39).

Changing Leadership:
When God transitions into a new era there is a general principle that the leadership of the Church comes under adjustment. This is caused by several reasons. Generally, the older leadership that has become comfortable in their positions tends to resist the coming of the new spiritual positions. This creates a tension in the ranks of leadership in the Body of Christ. Also the doctrine of the new truth is proclaimed and declared by a new group of revelatory preachers who come forth with a new dimension of authority. God never retreats to a lesser position of glory. Each new dimension of God comes forth with greater authority, clarity and power of proclamation. There is a gathering of people around this fresh dimension and so a movement is formed among the people. Just as God moved from Eli to Samuel, from Saul to David, from Moses to Joshua in order to bring His people into a deeper dimension of relationship and accomplishment of His purpose so He still does today.

It is important to realize that a change of leadership does not immediately mean that God rejects all the former leaders of the past moves. Many senior leaders of past moves transition into the new moves of God and in so doing they move from a 'position' of Moses to a 'position' of Joshua. The use of the terms Eli, Saul and Moses as representative of what God is moving from, refers to the position occupied in the Spirit by these past leaders not to the actual individuals themselves. God loves all His leaders and many keep active in useful and powerful ministry even if they do not transition to the most accurate position for the current time.

Changing Culture:
A new move of God usually causes a change of how the corporate community expresses itself in the corporate worship. New songs generally are composed to capture the new understandings of God that prevail in the midst of the move. The music of the Church generally is a powerful factor for determining the 'culture' and 'atmosphere' of the local church. The way in which we worship is representative of the vision we have captured of the

Lord. A fresh perspective of the Lord changes us (2 Corinthians 3:18).

New vocabulary is developed to capture the fresh understanding. Many people are at first uncomfortable with the language of a new move of the Lord. If we look back through the history of the Church each move of God has its own particular sound and emphasis of worship and also a vocabulary that expresses the mentality of the saints in the most accurate way.

Apostolic Kingdom Teaching:

Every new move of God produces fresh areas of emphasis in doctrine. The Pentecostal Movement, for example, brought with it an emphasis on the baptism in the Holy Spirit with speaking in tongues as the evidence of having received the baptism. This truth was always in the Word of God but was not generally taught to the people by the leaders of the time.

It is important to realize that doctrine determines the shape of the spiritual culture, the operating mentality and the activity of the Church. With the new doctrinal emphasis in the Pentecostal Movement, people sang different songs, the sound and language of the Church changed, the patterns of ministry of the pastors and elders changed and the approach to life changed in the saints. There developed a new emphasis on what became called the 'Rapture' of the Church. The same patterns of change exist in the midst of this new move of God today.

Apostolic Kingdom Ministry:

In a new move of God the patterns of ministering also undergo change. By ministering I mean the process by which spiritual resource in transferred into the lives of the saints on an individual level. In the Pentecostal Movement there was a great emphasis on the laying on of hands on the believers for healing, deliverance and the baptism of the Holy Spirit. All of this is biblical and should be practiced in the Church in every era of its operations. In the Prophetic Movement in the 1980's there came a great emphasis on delivering words of personal prophecy to the saints as a fresh pathway to release to them relevant divine resource for the building of their lives. In the present Apostolic Kingdom

Transition is a term impartation and has come to a place of great emphasis. There is great release of divine resource to the individual lives of the saints as the apostolic kingdom word that is impregnated with life-giving power is decreed and proclaimed over the lives of the saints (Romans 1: 11). Impartation is a major dimension of the apostolic.

It is important to note that each new move of God does not abandon and reject the prevailing ministry pattern of the move that has gone before but includes and practices it in the midst of the new move. Therefore, it is clear to see that each new move becomes stronger and more comprehensive in its spiritual operations.

CHAPTER XIV.
SYSTEMATIC KINGDOM APOSTOLIC ORDER

<u>The Kingdom suffers violence</u>
The church is under attack. A powerful persecution is under way, and many sheep have been scattered. But what I am hearing from "independents" are cries such as, "I'll never follow another man!" or "No man is going to tell me what to do!" or "Beware of any group that has a hierarchical governmental structure."

While a limited amount of wisdom may be in such thinking, these independents may be failing to see a very real problem because they are looking in only one direction. While they critically examine others, problems of equal or greater magnitude in the areas of ignorance of God's Word, of respect for government or gross intolerance for another's weaknesses may be in them.

They have reacted by divorcing themselves from any group and "floating" among many groups. Their attitude is such that, even when they do attend, they are in reality just passing through. It is very much like the modern practice of a man and woman living together without commitment. Each "takes" what they can get from the relationship, but one is always free to leave if things do not go quite as planned.

Daniel writes:
Then I heard the man clothed in linen, who was above the waters of the river, when he held up his right hand and his left hand to heaven, and swore by Him who lives forever, that it shall be for a time, times, and half a time; and when the <u>power of the</u>

holy people has been completely shattered *[scattered,* KJV], all these things shall be finished. (Daniel 12:7)

Surely the enemy has attacked, and the sheep are scattered! Jesus says, "And when he [the true shepherd] brings out his own sheep, he goes before them; and the sheep follow him, for they know his voice. Yet they will by no means follow a stranger, but will flee from him, for they do not know the voice of strangers. (John 10:4-5)

We had good reason to flee our former association: The voice of a stranger was heard within it, and we could not follow him. But is it possible that the "independents" still do not hear the True Shepherd's voice? Could they have fled for different reasons? This is why these people may be in very real danger. They cannot come to *any* shepherd because their confusion and governmental problems are preventing it.

The Church's mandate is based on the Scripture passage referred to as the Great Commission is found in Matthew 28:16-20.
1. The church is commanded to make disciples of all nations (v. 19)
2. The church is commanded to baptize it disciples (v. 19), which means being admitted, recognized, loved, and accepted into and by His church. Paul organized churches, he instructed them, cared for them, and visited them again and again. He admonished them to obey the Lord in their service to Him and in their spiritual growth. (Acts 15:36)
3. The church is commanded to teach its disciples to observe all things that Jesus commanded them (v.20).

Today as we enter the 21st century the Spirit of God is moving again and calling the Church forward out of Pentecostal/Charismatic/Prophetic positions into the new arena of the Apostolic Order. Two very powerful and important things highlight this move of God:

Firstly, it is activated by the release, presence and acceptance of the powerful impartation and revelation ministries of the church apostles being raised up and sent by the Lord to the earth today.

Secondly, it is a globally defined move of God. Major aspects of this God's Apostolic Order are being defined in sectors of the Church, which were previously perceived to be receptor or importer areas, and not distributor or exporter areas for divine truth.

For this move of God to be clearly received and defined in the earth, both the arrogance of some areas of the Church that previously held the monopoly on defined truth, and the mendicant and pathetic mentality of those in the Third World who never strongly expressed the uniqueness of God in them must be shattered (Luke 3: 4 . 6).

A God ordered move changes every characteristic and parameter of what went before. It is a structural and complete change of the entire operating system of the Church. In a transition, God moves radically to a higher degree of glory and purpose. He leaves nothing untouched by the new demand that we move closer to Him.

The direction of this transition is inward towards a stronger position of God in the hearts of men. Though in systematic change there may be mighty manifestations of the power of God, manifestation without inner restructuring is worthless. There is a greater proclamation of the power of the Kingdom manifesting in the earth, a higher understanding of the requirement of the Lord that we finish His work and purpose here in the earth as the prophets have spoken. There is developing a clear comprehension that we can no longer sit around in a self-centered, building-based Christianity waiting for Jesus to make His appearance. Now we comprehend that God has an ultimate purpose and plan. He cannot return until all His purposes are fulfilled. The way to the meeting with Christ is the forceful completion of His purposes in the earth in the character and power of the Spirit.

The new confidence that is arising in the Church is brought about by a fresh sense of partnership with Christ (1 Corinthians 3:9). It has brought to the Church a new level of warfare against the powers of darkness. It is impossible to exist today as a victorious believer and disciple of Christ without a realization that Satan is no longer our major problem. The more serious issue is the extent to which we are accurately walking in and fulfilling the plan of God. If we walk in His accurate will then all battles will be fought and won. We cannot be stopped if we submit to His direction and proceed in absolute obedience.

The coming of the Kingsom Apostolic order of God, with the release of the apostolic/prophetic spirit in the Church has banished the 'soft' spirit-culture of the Charismatic Move. We retain the inner spirit of adoration but we have moved to a much more manifest conquering position. Our praise and worship is full of the proclamations of the Lord. s victory within us moving out into our environment. Our prayer is now filled with prophetic declarations and apostolic decrees. The emphasis and focus is now no longer on a 'bless-me' position but has shifted radically to a martyr's position with the question: What can I do for the Lord?. Now we are truly SERVING Him.

Our local churches are no longer hide-outs for the rebellious, the religious and the disobedient. Senior pastors are rising up under the impartation of the apostolic grace brought to them through relationship with apostles and apostolic networks, to speak accurately the prophetic word from God to their community. New levels of divine order are coming into local churches as saints receive the demand of God and let Him into their hearts in a deeper way. Now the government of God truly starts from within and is manifested outward in spiritually balanced lifestyles that can enter deep into the purposes of God.

A cry for the nations is rising as a crescendo in the churches. We can no longer be denied our right to break out of the limitations imposed upon us by the enemy. Just as the early Israelites broke out from under Pharaoh by the power of the Moses impartation, so today the people of God are shattering all limitations under the power of the apostolic grace. Our heart is for the nations of the earth to be completely touched by the power of God. Lives must be transformed on a massive scale if we have to come to the end of God. s plan. The faith, understanding, courage, leadership, ability and prophetic discernment have all been provided in the ordered Apostolic Move of God for all this to be accomplished.

Making the Transition

We must all come to a clear realization that when God moves to a new position by His Spirit and releases new resources to His Church in the earth that we do not have an option to obey. WE MUST TRANSITION WITH GOD. The inner acceptance of the mandatory nature of transition is the beginning step to the process. The key to following the cloud as the early Israelites exited Pharaoh. s Egypt and began the journey was this simple truth: the cloud determined the rate and the frequency of the process. If the cloud remained in one place for a day then they stayed for a day. If it lingered for a year then they stayed for a year (Numbers 9: 22-23). The process was not regular. It occurred in pulses of spiritual activity at irregular intervals. Therefore the next journey could not be programmed. It required discernment and obedience to be able to follow the cloud to the new spiritual position. So it is with us today in the spiritual process.

Let me mention five (5) basic requirements for successful transition:

We must adjust our personal paradigm (Luke 5: 37-39)

The new wine must be poured into new wineskins. The old thought patterns and expectancy patterns cannot accommodate the new thing that God is doing. We must be willing to change. Verse 39 says that at first the old tastes better. Therefore the old ways seems to be more pleasant in the early days of transition. There may be things we do not understand at first; concepts that disrupt our expected patterns but we must persevere in moving towards understanding and competence in the new move of God.

We must seek out relevant information (Proverbs 2: 3-6)

Enlightened decisions about the important ministries we have received from the Lord must be based on accurate information. We must not reject . wisdom. (Current information about the current doings of the Lord) (Proverbs 21:16). Books, tapes, visit to relevant conferences, personal study of the Word received, discussion and consultation all form part of the process of knowledge acquisition upon which we base our decisive actions to participate in the transition. The Berean process is: RECEPTIVITY + VALIDATION = APPLICATION (Acts 17: 11-12)

Transition must be strategic action (Joshua 4: 3- 9)

Transition must take plan with planned activity. We must have a vision of where we are going and then devise a plan to get there. When Joshua led the people across the Jordan he instructed them to take up 12 stones from the bed of the river and to pile them up in the place where they spent the first night in the new land. Twelve is the apostolic number of government and decisive and accurate human action. Key to the process is that we do not ever go backward into mentalities from which we have departed. Joshua's apostolic monument would forever remind the people never to go backward to the past experience.

Beneficial relationships must be built and maintained (Proverbs 13: 20)

It is wise to company with those who are going in the same direction as you are. If the values that you seek reside in them then those values will prosper in your own spirit. It is important that all ministries moving into an apostolic paradigm seek to fellowship with the apostolic grace by relating to an accurate and God ordained apostolic network. As in al other things you should seek the Lord for His direction and for His preference for your joinings.

Recognize that transition is not instantaneous. It is a process.

The acceptance of the new thing of God within our heart may be instantaneous but the reality of full transition is a process that can take quite a while to come to full maturity in our lives. As a result we must neither be impatient nor must we abort the process through discouragement or laziness. The patterns of understanding and operation were built up in us over a fairly long period of time so that we cannot expect to 'reprogram. in an instant' Be consistent, be faithful, be open to the Spirit of the Lord, be enduring in your pursuit of knowledge, relationship, discernment and understanding and the fullness of all that God is releasing today will be birthed and matured within you.

The transition into a God mandated kingdom apostolic move has brought about the reform of doctrines and theology in a bid to clearly and accurately define scriptures in bringing a balance in line with the mind of Christ. This has created some dissentions. This dissent of revelation and theology has brought about a disagreement with the popular opinion of the majority. Basically revealed truth has been framed to be lies, especially with those of traditional up-bring that has dwelt in the world church for years.

In past moves of God, dissensions occurred yet in the fullness of time, revelation and reformation was accepted. Time is the key that unlocks revelation. So it will be with the present kingdom apostolic order of theology, eschatological doctrines and teachings. *However, it is important that we resound this that the apostolic movement is alive and well, and will accomplish the purpose of God in the Church and in the earth.* God will not defer reformation for any reason of our mental faculty or oblige to any form of human compromise and indulgence. If it be of the Spirit, no one will be able to resist the wisdom by which we speak.

If the present apostolic kingdom movement of theology is of God, no man or denomination will be able to resist the wisdom and the Spirit by which we speak. Though men and organizations are suborned against the truth and boldly say that apostolic order is migrating into error and apostasy, yet *the word will prevail* will only fail when it is false. I'm not saying that all that is being taught by the different streams of apostolic ministries and ministers are truth, as I recognize that many are being taking by the devil himself into high mountains and satan is giving them new revelations as well. See to it that you do not validate the false as well as not speak against the truth, least you enter into a fight with the program and purposes of God.

We should refrain from the God's mandated apostolic order if we do not have understanding of what it is. Do nothing against it and don't become critics, if what they are doing is something of their own, it will fail, but if it be of the Lord, we cannot stop it anyway, unless we want to fight against God.

Why do the heathen rage, and the people imagine a vain thing? The kings of the earth set themselves, and the rulers take counsel together, against the LORD, and against his anointed (Christ _ The Corporate Son), saying, Let us break their bands asunder, and cast away their cords from us. He that sitteth in the heavens shall laugh: the Lord shall have them in derision. Then shall he speak unto them in his wrath, and vex them in his sore displeasure . (Psalms 2:15).

Vain imaginations against Gods reformation are empty, fruitless and vain. Some will cling to the former things because of lack of understanding. *Think over (consider, reflect on or take into account) what I say, for the Lord will give you understanding in all things. (2 Timothy 2:7 New Revised Standard Version - emphasis added).*

The lack of understanding of the declaration of the apostolic reformation and the message of the Kingdom seems to be threatening the foundations of past moves and ministry establishments, and this has created a strong resistance against the movement. We need to think over (reconsider, reflect on or take into account) accurately the apostolic kingdom move and the revelations of the unveiled word. The more we understand the apostolic dimension and the message of the Kingdom, we will learn to appreciate and grasp the movement and become a part of this great last day shift of God.

Because of the lack of understanding and consideration, many are rejecting this great reformation and they are embracing the old order. The Holy Spirit will only reveal new things and unveil fresh revelations when we have an open mind to consider what is being said. If we are close-minded and judgmental of the apostolic reformation and the restoration of the apostles doctrines, then we will become hypercritical and remain stagnant without flowing with the Holy Spirit and what God is doing.

Kingdom Apostolic order has the grace and unique ability to execute and carry out the prophetic plans and purposes of God in finishing the kingdom work and commission upon the Church. Though the present Kingdom apostolic order is very confrontational in her bid to adjust and re-modify the mindset of Church leadership and the handling of the word. The present state of mind of the Church is bound in the traditions and cultures of religion. There is a strong eschatological ethnicity that captivates the attitude and the opinion of the way of thinking that must be fine-tuned. This is what apostolic order is all about. Our perspective and deportment is challenged in light of the apostolic revelation and doctrine.

But when I saw that they walked not uprightly according to the truth of the gospel, I said unto Peter before them all, If thou, being a Jew, livest after the manner of Gentiles, and not as do the Jews, why compellest thou the Gentiles to live as do the Jews? (Galatians 2:14).

In the absence of authentic apostolic ministry and order, the Church has been led from truth. There has been little precision in the word. Only few are willing to walk in candor (straightforwardness and forthrightness) of the word as modern day Pharisees gather against the present apostolic reformation.
This move of God is divinely mandated to declare a new word of revelation. The new word cannot be judged by the old word. The new word will manifest and establish the Kingdom of God in the earth.

These were more noble than those in Thessalonica, in that they received the word with all readiness of mind, and searched the scriptures daily, whether those things were so. Therefore, many of them believed; also of honorable women (Acts 17:11-12).

God's word endures and He will manifest His purpose in the earth. Openness of mind to receive and believe the word will result in confirmation of what God is saying in this present reformation. Be ready to lay aside doctrines that conflict with scripture. We do not look into the scripture in the light of our doctrine as it will bring a conflict with the word. Any doctrine that conflicts the scripture must be changed or lay aside, because it is wrong and dangerous.

The Kingdom message is not just educational, but it is maturational. God intends to grow us up and not just wanting to increase our knowledge. The Christ centered apostolic message of the Kingdom is a seasonal word that is relevant for the Body of Christ today. Though there is skepticism due to lack of understanding and the direction it seems to be going, but in due season, God will manifest His true purpose and agenda.

A breakthrough anointing is being released and no principality, nation or authority will stop the advancement of the Kingdom message. This anointing will tear down strongholds. God seeks to establish His Kingdom in the earth. The process of building in the Spirit involves a clear area (pulling down of strongholds) and a foundation upon which to build (apostles and prophets).

God is restoring apostles and the apostolic nature of the Church. *Becoming an apostolic people has to do with our attitude and lifestyle.* Some leaders speak about apostolic reformation but think institutionally rather than relationally. Apostolic people walk in relationship. Unless we build relationally, we cannot be apostolic people. Apostolic people walk in power, authority, signs and wonders. Beyond these, the nature of an apostle is that of humility, gentleness and love. The authority of the apostles come through submission.

The order of the Kingdom brings about an apostolic reconfiguration for the establishment of pragmatic truths in the Church. It is the release of present truths. There are past truths and present truths. If we are to come into the new things that God is doing, we need to leave behind past truths and come into the new day and season of God where present truths are released. *The Church must be established in present truth.* We have gone too far from true biblical order, truths and teachings and we have sought to establish our own traditional ecclesiastical order. This has affected the corporate Body and hinders the revelations of the purposes of God in the earth. One of the enemy and hindrance in seeing an apostolic order is the tradition of men and denominational doctrines that have been set in place. We need to begin to do things Gods way. *The pursuit of truth is the noblest responsibility that we have during this reformation season.*

As apostolic people, we must become purposely placed in Gods word and become spiritually balanced. Effective apostolic and prophetic ministry, as , well as other ministry gifts must communicate balanced revelation truths and build upon the foundation that has been laid, with Jesus being the chief cornerstone. Apostolic and prophetic ministries must have its foundation on the word. Not just reading or studying the word, but understanding the mysteries of Christ and of the Kingdom and be able to communicate present truths.

Wherefore the rather, brethren, give diligence to make your calling and election sure: for if ye do these things, ye shall never fall: For so an entrance shall be ministered unto you abundantly into the everlasting kingdom of our Lord and Savior Jesus Christ. Wherefore I will not be negligent to put you always in remembrance of these things, though ye know them, and be established in the present truth. (2 Peter 1:10-12).

The kingdom apostolic transition is still going through the process of establishment, maturity and perfection; and we should not give ourselves to the errors and mistakes of the past leaders and moves. One of the key defects to present truths is that they have been taught by so many leaders who have no basic understanding of the Kingdom and the purposes of God for the earth at this time. The apostolic transition must bring a clear distinction in structure and function for Kingdom advancement. If we continue to speak of what we do not know or have an understanding and revelation of, then we will produce nothing of accomplishment and quality in the earth that is of God.

A development of our spirit man is required to be able to hear and communicate with God and His people. The purpose of God cannot be made clear to us if we are still spiritually immature as we cannot comprehend them. The Church of God must not be led by children, but by men and women who understand the principles of spiritual leadership in this present season of reformation.

Yet we do speak wisdom among those who are mature; a wisdom, however, not of this age nor of the rulers of this age, who are passing away; but we speak God's wisdom in a mystery, the hidden wisdom which God predestined before the ages to our glory; the wisdom which none of the rulers of this age has understood; for if they had understood it they would not have crucified the Lord of glory; but just as it is written, "THINGS WHICH EYE HAS NOT SEEN AND EAR HAS NOT HEARD, AND WHICH HAVE NOT ENTERED THE HEART OF MAN, ALL THAT GOD HAS PREPARED FOR THOSE WHO LOVE HIM." For to us God revealed them through the Spirit; for the Spirit searches all things, even the depths of God. For who among men knows the thoughts of a man except the spirit of the man which is in him? Even so the thoughts of God no one knows except the Spirit of God. (1 Corinthians 2:6-11 NAS 1995 Edition).

The people will not be able to progress and grow beyond where they are if we do not have matured and full-fledged apostolic leaders to teach them the whole counsel of God and feed meat to them. What we have seen is a constant feeding on milk and our milk diet has caused a deficiency and paucity in the present transition. Too many boy-leaders and very few matured apostolic leaders. We cannot impart the next generation with that which we do not have; neither can we take the people of God beyond our present level.

We need strong apostolic and prophetic leadership that are able to stand in the heat of the battle and wage a good warfare of faith. We need to learn how to build in the Spirit and effectively pull down the strongholds of the enemy. Chocolate soldiers (ones who cannot endure) will melt in the heat of the spiritual battle.

It is important that the apostolic message and the revelation of the Kingdom should be simplified and made plain, so that the common and immature leaders and believers alike can grasp the truth with clear and accurate understanding. Much of our new developed terminology and spiritual technology must be broken down to a simple understandable form, and enough time should be given to fully and clearly explain and impart present truth. We cannot just brush through the surface of a new revealed revelation and truth and expect everyone to know what we are saying. I think this is part of the problem of the leadership of the Church.

Apostolic leaders that have made full transition into the new move of God and into another level should be very careful not to become a hindrance to those who are yet to make the transition and to those who are still yet to move into a new level. Our attitude and approach to them should be that of love and patience. We should not be egotistical and too authoritative, so that we don't destroy, rather than building; especially when it is outside our local ministry where we do not have the time to really sat down and systematically build and develop the people through the transition process.

In the midst of true and authentic kingdom apostolic transformation, there are the classification of those I call parrot mouth ministers and ministries taking upon themselves the cloth of a reformer. They know how to duplicate and talk like a parrot, but cannot express the lifestyle or manifest the grace, and as a result they cannot impart anything of the mysteries of the life and stature of Christ. All they are good for is to access materials through means of modern technology, but they cannot really define revealed truth as they lack the power thereof.

We cannot be apostolic if we do not possess the Spirit, grace and character of a five-fold ministry minister; even though we speak like them and associate ourselves in the company of apostolic leaders. You will only have a Saul spirit who's anointing flows from the purification and demands of men, rather than from the true source; this will result to your house getting weaker and weaker against the house of David who is a true reflection of the apostolic change that is after Gods own heart. We cannot line in an apostolic dimension unless we have an apostolic grace. We cannot function without the grace.

There are certain characteristics that give a trademark to the Church that is walking in God's Apostolically ordered maturity according to **Ephesians 4:11-16.**

1. They have fully accepted and are walking in the complete potential of the restored and established five-fold ministry.
2. They are doing the work of the ministry.
3. They walk in the unity of the faith.
4. They are established in the knowledge of the Son of God (having received sonship) and walk in the ' Apostles doctrine.
5. They are not tossed and carried about by all kinds of teachings. They are no longer influenced by people who use cunning and clever strategies to lead them astray.
6. They speak the truth in love.
7. They are united in the Body and fit together through the support of every joint. Every part does its job and makes the Body grow (increase) so that it builds up and edifies itself in love.

CHAPTER XV.
KINGDOM APOSTOLIC ORDER

If we could understand the dynamics of what God intended in the beginning, then we would make better sense of where we are now and where we need to be going. *Intent* can be defined as original purpose. It is more important for us to know what a person intended than to know what was actually said or done. If we do not properly discern intent, misunderstanding will follow. This is one reason why there are so many confused people in the world: We have misunderstood God's original intent; we have misunderstood not only ourselves, but also God's purpose for us on Earth.

Understanding intent expands our capacity to realize God's overall plan. When we see or hear only a small portion of the whole, we will misunderstand and draw an incorrect conclusion. God has a purpose for everything He does. All of us who are of His Kingdom are part of His overall plan, but often all we can only glimpse that which involves us at any given moment is a partial plan. Constantly relying on the Bible as God's instruction for life in His Kingdom, will aware of His intent, which will, in turn, lead us and keep us focused. Intent is also the most critical component of motivation. It is the source of motivation and the reason why someone does something or creates something. Unless specifically stated, however, intent is usually hidden.

God's original intent—and His continuing purpose—was and is to extend His invisible heavenly Kingdom to the Earth, to influence Earth from Heaven through the rulership of His earthly children created in His image. The expansion of a kingdom government (or any government) from one place to another by planting an outpost in that new place is called colonization, and the outpost so planted is called a colony. Simply stated, God's original intent was to establish Kingdom Apostolic Order.

One reason that Christ's *ekklesia* has not made more of an impact in the world is because too many Kingdom citizens have accommodated and adapted to the culture of the world instead of maintaining the culture of our home government. We have neglected our "apostolic mandate" become overrun with worldly teachings. There are two kinds of people in the world: those who are children of the Kingdom of Heaven, and those who are not. Christ Himself made this distinction clear in a teaching story He told about a farmer who planted good seed in his field. (Matt. 13:24-36)

Strangely enough, the single biggest cause of our problems is the very thing that was supposed to provide a solution: religion. Historically, religion has been the primary driving force behind the vast majority of global conflict. This is especially true today. Global terrorism is fueled by extremist religious ideology. In the name of Allah, radical Muslim groups such as Hamas and al-Qaida utilize violence and terror to either convert or destroy the " infidels" (unbelievers). In Iraq, Sunni and Shiite Muslims kill each other in a bloodletting unleashed by the release of years of pent-up anger, resentment, hostility, and hatred. The burning of churches in Pakistan results in the retaliatory torching of temples and mosques in India.

Religion is *not* a peaceful prospect, and religious conflict is not restricted to Islam or Hinduism or other " non-Western" religions. Christianity carries its own heavy burden of responsibility for religiously motivated conflict. The Crusades of the Middle Ages and centuries of hostility and persecution between Catholics and Protestants are two prime examples. Think of all the years that Belfast and Northern Ireland burned with unrest and violence because Catholics and Protestants were unable to live together in peace. Denominations within the Church are like little kingdoms of their own, jockeying for position and advantage and fighting amongst themselves over theology, doctrine, and theories of church government instead of working together for the common cause of the Gospel. This is why I make a clear and unambiguous distinction between the Apostolic Kingdom order and institutional Christianity as a religious entity.

Jesus Christ preached the Gospel of the Kingdom, which was His primary reason for coming. But His Kingdom message would mean nothing unless the sin that separated all people from God was removed. The Holy Spirit could not inhabit a sin-soiled vessel. So Jesus completed His mission by dying on a cross, shedding His sinless blood to save, or salvage us and restore us to a right relationship with our heavenly Father. The Gospel, or " good news," is not only the blood of Jesus, but also the message of the Kingdom of Heaven—that it has arrived and is available for all to enter. The blood of Jesus is the cleansing agent that we must pass through in order to make our " house" clean so that the Governor can take up residence. The death of Christ on the cross was absolutely necessary because " [God's] *law requires that nearly everything be cleansed with blood, and without the shedding of blood there is no forgiveness*" (Heb. 9:22).

The Bible says that all of us have sinned and fallen short of God's righteous standard (see Rom. 3:23). Sin is rebellion against God, which separated us from Him and made the " houses" of our lives dirty and unholy, unfit for the presence of a holy Governor. The sinless blood of Jesus has the power to thoroughly cleanse our house and make it holy again.

In reading the four Gospels of the New Testament—Matthew, Mark, Luke, and John—it becomes immediately clear that Jesus used two similar but different phrases to refer to the country of the King and the influence of the King. Sometimes He referred to the " Kingdom of Heaven," and at other times to the " Kingdom of God."

Although it is common to use these phrases interchangeably, there is an important difference in focus. The phrase " Kingdom of Heaven" refers to the literal place, the " headquarters" country of God. " Kingdom of God," on the other hand, refers to the King's influence wherever it extends, but especially its extension into the earthly realm. Another way to explain the distinction is to say that while we can *go* to the Kingdom of Heaven, we can *bring* the Kingdom of God to the Earth. Heaven is the place; the Kingdom of God is the influence. That is why Jesus said, " *The kingdom of God is within you*" (Luke

17:21b). Wherever the Kingdom of God is, the Kingdom of Heaven has influence. So, wherever we go as Kingdom citizens, the influence of the King should go along.

Jesus taught His disciples to pray, but we need to keep returning to it because it is also His Kingdom model prayer:

> *Our Father in heaven, hallowed be Your name, Yourkingdom come, Your will be done on earth as it is inheaven* (Matthew 6:9b-10).

"On earth as it is in heaven": that is our number one prayer. We should not pray for retreat. We should not pray for rescue. We should pray for *revolution*. Every time we pray for God to take us out of the world, we are praying the wrong prayer. Instead, we should pray for Heaven to come to Earth—for His Garden to spread until it fills the planet.

One of the words for *prayer* in the New Testament also means " petition." A petition is a legal act. It is used to address a government. Often, when we read the word *prayer* in the New Testament, it is talking about petitioning. You only petition government. For many believers, prayer does not work the way it should because they have made it a religious exercise of pleading for a favor rather than a legal act of asserting their rights and privileges as Kingdom citizens. Prayer is business with the government of God. It is where we bring a legal claim to legitimate government authority and demand the government's response.

God's desire is to build a heavenly community on Earth through the cultivation of His Kingdom culture here. This is exemplified both in the prayer of Jesus: " *Your kingdom come, Your will be done on earth as it is in heaven*" (Matt. 6:10), and in the plan of God from the beginning: " *Let Us make man in Our image...and let them rule...*" (Gen. 1:26). God doesn't want a religion. He doesn't want a weekend ceremony. He isn't looking for a group of weird people dressed in weird clothes saying weird things. God wants a holy community of whole and complete citizens, a community that represents and reflects Heaven on Earth, and He wants to do it through cultivating His Kingdom's culture on Earth through the lives and influence of His people.

Some churches and denominational groups have started lowering their standard of values in order to attract more people. Surrendering to political correctness and social pressures, they are adjusting their theology and their doctrine to accommodate personal perversion and give it dignity. The Bible says that those who do such things have no inheritance in the Kingdom of God. In contrast, the Kingdom of God never lowers its standards of value to accommodate anyone's personal preferences. Instead, it challenges people to adjust their preferences to come into alignment with the Kingdom's standards. In effect, the King has said, " Here are the standards for life in My Kingdom. Compliance is mandatory; otherwise, you don't come in."

THE dynamics of transformation involves influencing the popular culture through the community of faith. All humans are searching for meaning in their lives. We all want to know that there is a reason and a purpose for our existence; that we were not born by accident.

Throughout the ages, human philosophers have sought to understand life and therefore find meaning in it. Religion has tried to do the same thing. Regardless of their culture, people all over the world look at their surroundings and circumstances and ask, " Is this all?" They examine their day-to-day experiences and think, " Certainly there is more to life than this."

By and large, however, man's search for meaning has come up empty because he has failed or refused to look for meaning and purpose in the one place in the universe he can find them: in the community of God's people. As Kingdom citizens and members of the Kingdom community, we not only possess the answer to humanity's search for meaning, but we also bear the responsibility of sharing it with others.

The only way for the church to bring its influence to bear in the world is by engaging the popular culture on equal terms on a consistent, day-by-day basis. In order to do this, we must each be committed to representing the nature and character of our Lord and Savior by living His culture daily before the world with boldness and without apology or compromise. Man's search for meaning is all about his quest for a lost inheritance. Philosophy can't find it. Science can't find it. Religion can't find it. Only those who are chosen by God and of the Kingdom of Heaven have found it, because the King, Jesus Christ, Himself has restored it. In fact, the Kingdom itself is the inheritance, and with the Kingdom comes everything else.

Possession of the inheritance is what distinguishes the Kingdom children of God and body from all other communities and peoples on Earth. The King desires for every person in the world to become a citizen of His community and to receive his or her inheritance. The day is coming when the King Himself will separate forever those who are His from those who are not. In the meantime, He has charged His beloved ones with the commission to engage the world and proclaim His Kingdom by both word and lifestyle so that as many as possible of the people of the world will transfer their citizenship from the Kingdom of darkness to the Kingdom of God.

Although we will not experience the complete fullness of our inheritance until we enter the life to come, as Kingdom citizens, our inheritance is a present reality. In fact, Kingdom community life is the daily living out of our inheritance in real and practical ways. Jesus described it this way:

When the Son of man comes in His glory, and all the angels with Him, He will sit on His throne in heavenly glory. All the nations will be gathered before Him, and He will separate the people one from another as a shepherd separates the sheep from the goats. He will put the sheep on His right and the goats on His left. Then the king will say to those on His right, "Come, you who are blessed by My Father; take your inheritance, the kingdom prepared for you since the creation of the world. For I was hungry and you gave Me something to eat, I was thirsty and you gave Me something to drink, I was a stranger and you invited Me in, I needed clothes and you clothed Me, I was sick and you looked after Me, I was in prison and you came to visit Me."

Then the righteous will answer Him, "Lord, when did we see You hungry and feed You, or thirsty and give You something to drink? When did we see You a stranger and invite You in, or needing clothes and clothe You? When did we see You sick or in prison and go to visit You?"

The King will reply, "I tell you the truth, whatever you did for one of the least of these brothers of Mine, you did for Me" (Matthew 25:31-40).

We have not inherited a religion. Cultures and societies may transfer religions from one generation to the next, but that is not our inheritance. Our inheritance is the Kingdom—not just any kingdom, but *the* Kingdom. What Adam lost, Christ has restored to us. Rulership is in our genes, authority, in our very makeup. We were designed to rule the Earth. The Kingdom is the rightful inheritance of all humankind. Many people, however, do not know this, which is why we of the Kingdom community must engage those who live in the world's culture. They need to be informed of their inheritance.

As Kingdom citizens, our goal should be to stay in touch with the Holy Spirit to hear what our Father is saying concerning apostolic order every moment of every day. It is for this reason that God sent His Holy Spirit not to visit us but to live inside of us, so He could guide us into the knowledge of all truth and teach us how to live and act and talk like the Him. This is the way—and the only way—for us to exert a continuing influence and make a permanent impact for the Kingdom in the popular culture. In order to transform the popular culture, we must engage the popular culture, and we can engage it successfully only in the Spirit, likeness, and power of our God.

ENGAGING THE WORLD IS OUR PRIORITY

God did not place us on Earth as His people just so we could start getting ready to leave. He placed us here to plant and reproduce of His Apostolic Kingdom throughout the world, thereby reclaiming and transforming territory laid waste by the pretender's rapacious rule. Having examined what we were *not* assigned to do, it is time to look more specifically at the assignments our King *has* given us.

Here is what we are *supposed* to be doing.
1. *God assigned us to reintroduce the Kingdom to the world to His apostolic order.*

Jesus set the stage. He laid the groundwork when He first appeared in His public ministry proclaiming a simple, straightforward message: "*Repent, for the kingdom of heaven is near*" (Matt. 4:17). He called followers to Himself and established His Church, His *ekklesia*, His " called-out ones," to continue the work He began, to preach the same message, and to carry out the same assignment. That is why He told His disciples,

I tell you the truth, anyone who has faith in Me will do what I have been doing. He will do even greater things than these, because I am going to the Father (John 14:12).

People all over the world are searching for the Kingdom even though they don't know it. We who are of the Kingdom bear the responsibility of helping them find it. Our assignment is linked to the timing of Christ's return and the end of the age:

"And this gospel of the kingdom will be preached in the whole world as a testimony to all nations, and then the end will come" (Matt. 24:14).

God assigned us to repossess the earth with the Kingdom. Psalm 24:1 says, "*The earth is the Lord's, and everything in it, the world, and all who live in it.*" Psalm 115:16
adds, "*The highest heavens belong to the Lord, but the earth He has given to man.*"

These verses are still true because God never changes, and His gifts and calling are irrevocable (see Rom. 11:29).

2. *Yet for thousands of years the Earth effectively has been under the rule and sway of satan.* Christ's death and resurrection broke satan's power and put him on notice of eviction. He restored and reconciled back to the Father on earth to its rightful human overlords. Now, like the ancient Israelites after they crossed the Jordan River to take possession of the land of Canaan, as God had promised, it is time for us as Kingdom citizens to fully repossess the territory that is rightfully ours. We do this not by separation but by infiltration.

3. *God assigned us to engage the world system.* Engagement means involvement. Battles in wartime are often called engagements. To engage something means to meet it head on, to confront it and challenge it without backing down and without surrender. Popular society and culture will never be changed by those who refuse to engage them. It

has been said that all that is necessary for evil to triumph is for good people to do nothing. Evil has held sway in the world for far too long. People need to know that life has meaning and purpose. They need to know that there is an alternative to the seemingly unending cycle of hatred, violence, cruelty, poverty, and misery.

They need to be given reason for hope. Our assignment is to infuse the popular culture with the values, morals, and standards of the God's Apostolic Kingdom order. One way to do this is by working diligently for the passage of laws that uphold standards, and for the election of public officials who will do the same. The reason is simple: whoever controls the laws controls the culture. That is why the first thing God did after delivering the Israelites from Egyptian slavery was to give them a code of law. In order to make them into a nation, He needed to reshape their slave culture and mindset into the culture and mindset of people of God. Our purpose in engaging the world system is the same.

4. *God assigned us to influence the world, not to keep up with it.* It is impossible to change a culture by accommodating it.

Yet that is exactly what countless churches and believers have tried to do, to their own detriment. The only thing we accomplish by accommodating culture is to become like the very culture we are trying to change. Rather than transforming culture, when we accommodate, we allow the popular culture to transform us into its own image.

The secret to effective influence is to remain distinct. The standards and principles of the Kingdom of Heaven are diametrically opposed to those of the world system. When people in that system see Apostolic Kingdom communities where Kingdom citizens are living according to God's principles, the difference will be so stark as to be unmistakable. And when they see that kingdom communities actually work, and bring about an environment and lifestyle of peace, joy, contentment, and prosperity unlike anything found in the world, they will find it irresistible.

CHANGING THE SYSTEMS OF THIS WORLD

Our assignment is nothing less than to change the world; and to do that, we have to become involved with the world.

    5. *God assigned us to affect change in the world, not reject the world.*

When humankind chose to disobey God and reject His rule, God would have been perfectly within His rights as Creator to reject us, destroy us, and start all over. But He did not do that. He chose to pursue us in spite of our sin and woo and win us back to Him; and He did this by direct involvement.

Through His Son Jesus Christ, the King injected Himself directly into the world system, to change it not by war and conquest, but by influence, by the gradual infiltration and manifestation of His power and presence in the lives of individuals. Jesus went directly and deliberately to the castoffs of society, the people whom even the religious leaders—*especially* the religious leaders—wanted nothing to do with. He related to each one on a personal basis. In the same way, we are to spread Kingdom influence throughout the world—one person at a time.

    6. *God assigned us to revolutionize the world.*

As Kingdom citizens we are revolutionaries, because our Lord was a revolutionary. Christ never led an armed revolt against the Romans, but His life and teachings were revolutionary in their effect. Unlike other revolutionaries, however, who always seek to establish new ideas, Jesus' goal was to reestablish an *old* idea, God's original big idea of Heaven on Earth. His strategy was to employ words rather than warfare and influence instead of invasion. This is why He commonly made statements like: " You have heard that it was said…but I tell you…." He was applying a corrective. He was replacing bad ideas with good ideas and wrong thinking with right thinking. True revolutions begin by changing people's thinking; only then do they translate to action. We will change the world the same way: by the word, example, and influence.

    7. *God assigned us to occupy the Earth, not abandon it.*

God created the Earth to be inhabited, and He created us in His own image to be its inhabitants. His original mandate to us, which has never changed, was that we be fruitful and multiply, and that we fill the Earth and subdue it; in short, that we exercise dominion over it. So far, our overall track record under the pretender's influence has not been good, as we have abused and misused the Earth, its resources, its creatures, and our fellow humans. The purpose of Apostolic Kingdom communities, is to establish God's intended apostolic order here, and to correct and reverse that history. Our assignment is to occupy the Earth and fill it a new with the vibrant culture of God's order, God's government, God's intent, which gives life and purpose and value to everything it touches.

When Inner City Full Gospel was established, the foundational scripture that God gave was and is Ephesians 2:19-22. We did not know at that time that our ministry was an apostolic/prophetic ministry. My husband, Bishop M. A. Smith, has been operating in the office of the prophet since he was baptized and filled with the Holy Ghost. As he began to establish churches and impart to others it became apparent that he also has an apostolic anointing. Every year at our conference the Holy Spirit would lead us to do things on the level of global ministry. When you have an apostolic prophetic anointing the Holy Spirit shows you how to impart to others and to freely give what has been freely received. We would receive revelation from God of what to expect in the coming year, and give instructions to the people of God on how to prepare for what was coming.

There is a difference between lay pastor and an apostolic pastor. Don't have to be an apostle to have an apostolic anointing. An apostolic anointing is an anointing to increase and grow ministry or whatever they put your hands to do. Your connections determine your direction. The anointing is the Holy Spirit coming upon you to equip you for divine service. When you're in the presence of the Lord, the Holy Spirit drives the service. God does not anoint flesh works. (self made). God is not responsible for or to take care of illegitimate ministry. When a ministry is birthed out of prayer, that makes it legitimate. Your ministry is not to be imitated. Most of us look at big ministries, and desire a large building. Whenever you attract favor those who have abused and persecuted you will come back and ask a favor.

BIBLIOGRAPHY

Beausay, William, II. (1978). The Leadership Genius of Jesus. Nashville: Thomas Nelson

Brown, Colin. (1999) New International Dictionary of New Testament Theology. Volume I, Grand Rapids; Zondervan.

Conradie, Ernst M. (1999). In Search of a Vision of Hope for a New Century. Journal of Religion and Society, Volume 1 (1999)

Couch, Mal. (2006). A Biblical Theology of Church. NY: Kregel

Dennett, E. (1982). The Writings of Edward Dennett: God's Order. NY: Stem Publishing.

Dodd, C. H. (1964). The Apostolic Preaching and Its Developments. NY: Harper and Row.

Ehrhardt, Arnold. (1953). The Apostolic Succession in the First Two Centuries of the Church.

Enns, Paul. (1989). The Moody Handbook of Theology. IL: Moody Press.

Erickson, Millard J. Christian Theology. IL: Moody Press.

Hendricks, Obery. M., Jr. (2003). <u>The Politics of Jesus.</u> NY: Doubleday.

Hodges, Charles. (1995). <u>Systematic Theology</u>. MI: Eerdmans, reprinted.

Holmes, Michael W. (1997). <u>Apostolic Fathers.</u> NY: Baker

Johnson, Paul. (1976). <u>A History of Christianity</u>. NY: Athenium

Kent, Charles F. (1916). <u>The Work and Teachings of the Apostles.</u> NY: Schriber/sons

Kung, Hans. (1971). Papal Ministry in the Church

Pelican, Jasolas. (1971). <u>The Christian Tradition: A History of the Development of Doctrine.</u> University of Chicago.

Ryrie, Charles C. (1995). <u>Dispensationalism</u>. IL. Moody Press.

Vine, William E. (1985).Vine's Expository Dictionary of Biblical Words, An Expository Dictionary of New Testament Words with their Precise Meanings for English Readers, copyright 1985, p. 102.

William, Cave. (2007). <u>History of the Christian Church.</u> (www.ccel.org/s/schaff/history)

Willmington, H. L. Dr. (1995) <u>Willmington's Guide to the Bible.</u> Sri Lanka.

Wuest, Kenneth S. (1999) <u>Word Studies in the Greek New Testament. Volume I.</u>
Grand Rapids: Eerdsman. (pgs. 96-101).

SUGGESTIONS, QUESTIONS AND THOUGHTS

1. Ask Holy Spirit to open your understanding and give you Grace to receive, teach and train about Kingdom Apostolic Order.

2. Gather your leaders to discern what Apostolic Five-Fold ministry office they operate. Remember; the office is constant, vs. the gift.

3. Study what's Jesus' message of the Kingdom. Compare your teachings and sermons. Incorporate Kingdom principles into your teachings and sermons.

4. Teach, preach, and train your congregation about Kingdom citizenship, and benefits.

5. Does your doctrinal knowledge include solutions instead of contentions and quarrels?

6. What are your church's strengths? What authority is your church's structure founded?

7. What is the doctrine of the New Testament Church?

8. What denomination did the Apostles establish? What Scripture backs this up?

9. What is Kingdom Apostolic Order?

10. What is the temple structure plan for the church?

11. What is the foundation on which church should be grounded?

12. What is the church's mission vs. commission?

13. Who or what was behind Paul's inspiration?

14. How and why did Paul distinguish only two kinds of ministry?

15. What is the commission of your church? Is it Apostolic? Why?

16. What are the attributes of a sent one?

17. **What Scripture defines instruction for Apostolic order in the church?**

18. What portion of the Epistles are called pastoral and deal with church polity, policies, and practices?

19. What is the primary and essential need for the church to function as God designed?

20. Why can we not separate God's principles from His Apostolic practices?

21. The organic and unified growth of a church is based on-----?

22. For what purposes did Paul write the Epistle Titus?

23. What is the role of Holy Spirit in the church?

24. What does Scripture say about the church regarding denominations and organizations?

25. Explain what I Corinthians 1:10-13 implies and means? **Keep this Scripture in the foremost of your mind.**

26. What figure of speech describes the church Christ established?

27. What is the one word that Christ emphasized in His prayer in John 17?

28. What is God's Kingdom Apostolic Order for His church?

29. What is God's plan for your ministry according to His will?

30. How is God's nature expressed in the Church?

31. Who nudges us when change should occur?

32. Why do church leaders need the Apostolic Anointing of God's Spirit?

33. What are the prevailing attitudes seen in some believers as well as non-believers?

34. What does Jesus mean in Mark 7:8-9 concerning tradition? What describes good tradition?

35. Explain God's order according to Acts 5:29?

36. Which traditions appeuled to Jesus and why?

37. What changes produced scattering of the sheep?

38. What is the difference between the unity at the tower of Babel vs. oneness in I Cor. 1:10-13?

39. What tool does God use to accomplish His purpose on Earth?

40. What must the Church do to align with the authentic purpose of God? What must your church do?

41. How should God's Mandate be presented to your congregation?

42. What are the characteristics of true Godly Kingdom Apostolic Order?

43. What are the requirements for transitioning into Kingdom Apostolic Order?

44. **What are the assignments our Savior has given us for His Church.**

45. **Are you sure your doctrinal teaching and preaching align with God's Intended Apostolic Order for His Church?**

It is my hope and sincere desire that we the Church hear, listen and obey what the Spirit is saying. It's time for change.

www.ingramcontent.com/pod-product-compliance
Lightning Source LLC
Chambersburg PA
CBHW052056110526
44591CB00013B/2230